A-Z of Hell
Ross Kemp's
How Not to Travel the World

CENTURY

Published by Century 2014

2 4 6 8 10 9 7 5 3 1

Copyright © Ross Kemp 2014

Ross Kemp has asserted his right under the Copyright, Designs
and Patents Act 1988 to be identified as the author of this work

Every effort has been made to contact the copyright holders. The publishers will be
glad to correct any errors or omissions in future editions.

This book is a work of non-fiction based on the life, experiences and recollections of the
author. In some limited cases names of people, places, dates, sequences or the detail of
events have been changed solely to protect the privacy of others. The author has
stated to the publishers that, except in such minor respects not affecting the
substantial accuracy of the work, the contents of this book are true.

First published in Great Britain in 2014 by
Century
Random House, 20 Vauxhall Bridge Road,
London SW1V 2SA

www.randomhouse.co.uk

Addresses for companies within The Random House Group Limited can be found at:
www.randomhouse.co.uk

The Random House Group Limited Reg. No. 954009

A CIP catalogue record for this book
is available from the British Library

ISBN 9781780891910

The Random House Group Limited supports the Forest Stewardship
Council® (FSC®), the leading international forest-certification organisation.
Our books carrying the FSC label are printed on FSC®-certified paper.
FSC is the only forest-certification scheme supported by the leading
environmental organisations, including Greenpeace.
Our paper procurement policy can be found at:
www.randomhouse.co.uk/environment

Printed and bound by CPI Group (UK) Ltd, Croydon, CR0 4YY

Introduction

My dedicated team and I have been making documentaries for nigh-on ten years now and during that time we've become incredibly close, fallen out, made up, laughed, cried and come face to face with some of the very worst aspects of humanity. One thing I know for sure, I wouldn't be here now five coffees down and four kitkats to the good if it wasn't for that team. I want to thank them all from the bottom of my heart, and everyone at Sky for giving us the freedom and support to make the films we want to make.

As I sit here writing with my editor Ben Dunn looking over my shoulder, I remember that I originally wanted to call this book the *A-Z of What Not to Do*. Because given the option of doing the right or the wrong thing, I have generally chosen the latter. And, amazingly, most of those bad decisions have happened off the screen. So this book hopefully captures those moments you don't see on TV.

However, as you can tell, I often don't get my own way (others may disagree), so my editor insisted we call it the *A-Z of Hell* for 'commercial reasons'. So if you have purchased this book, he was right and I was wrong; if you haven't then I was wrong again.

Whatever's on the front cover, this book is an honest, sometimes tragic and at times (hopefully) amusing account of what happens when a hyperactive fortysomething-year-old man gets given the opportunity to travel the world and make documentaries. And as far as I'm concerned, long may it continue.

Ross Kemp, Ben Dunn's office, Penguin Random House, Pimlico 18.21 25 February 2014

A is for *'Avez-Vous Le Boeuf?'*

Grade Two CSE is the extent of my French, but even so I know what '*Avez-vous le boeuf?*' meant. It meant a pair of hungry, angry and possibly stoned Congolese guys were coming to get me.

Or at least it did on the night in question.

We were in the east of the Democratic Republic of the Congo for a film in the second series of *Extreme World*. It was the first time I'd returned to a genuine war zone since Afghanistan, and it would prove to be an eye-opening, not to mention distressing experience, mainly because of the sexual violence associated with the war. Not only is the war in the Congo the bloodiest conflict since the end of the Second World War, with around 6 million dead since 1998, but almost 400,000 women are raped there every year. Horrifically, brutally raped. It is, according to the UN, the rape capital of the world.

It's ironic how many countries with 'Democratic' in their name – many of which I've been to – clearly aren't.

Because the eastern DRC is technically a war zone there are no commercial flights in and out, so we had to reach it by road from neighbouring Rwanda. That was fitting, because it's in Rwanda that the roots of the Congolese conflict lie – the immediate roots, anyway – when, in 1994, during an attempted genocide that shocked the world, the Hutu tribe tried to ethnically cleanse Rwanda of Tutsis.

The Tutsis rose up against the Hutus and forced two million of them – including some of the ringleaders of the original uprising – to flee the country. And where did they go? They took the same road we did when we made our way from Rwanda into the eastern Democratic Republic of the Congo.

It was quite a journey, going from one country where the fighting and barbarism has drawn to a close into another where it continues to rage to this day. In terms of the change from one to the other it was like leaving Switzerland and finding yourself in Hades, for as we drove around the outskirts of Lake Kivu, still in Rwanda, we saw no signs of conflict. No barbed wire, no rubble, no half-demolished homes. Not even the piles of plastic you seem to encounter everywhere else in Africa.

Then we entered the Congo. And what a difference: rubbish, barbed wire and rubble were everywhere. We'd seen very few guns in Rwanda but here in the Congo it seemed as though every other guy was carrying: the Congolese police, army, UN peacekeeping troops in their distinctive blue helmets. We're talking about the largest deployment of UN troops in the world in the Congo and there were a *lot* of guns being carried around.

By the time we reached the border crossing, we were already mourning the comparative beauty of Rwanda. We clambered down from our Land Cruisers at a white, old colonial French-style building and I wandered up to a couple of bored-looking cops in shades (see K is for Kit).

'*Bonjour*,' I said, smiling. '*Ça va?*'

The cops scowled and led us around the back of the building to an office, where they quizzed us about the reasons for our visit. We're journalists, we told them. We're trying to do a story on the Congo.

What story? What story?

Absolutely paranoid, these guys, like something from *The Deer Hunter*, wanting to know what story we were planning to cover. Not far away was a grill, thick bars in the ground with hands poking through and prisoners inside babbling away in pidgin English. I'd heard them when we passed: 'Help me, help me,' and I'd looked at them nervously, feeling a mix of sympathy and a keen sense of not wanting to join them down there, fully aware we were being treated with extreme suspicion by the cops.

You could hardly blame them. The tribal problems in the Congo are made worse by the fact that it's so mineral rich. If you use a laptop, a mobile phone or a computer game then you're making use of coltan and cassiterite that may well have been mined in the Congo. Two-thirds of the world's coltan comes from the Congo, in fact.

You'd hope that sitting on top of huge reserves of minerals used by the vast majority of the Western world would be a good thing for the regular Congolese? And that some of the wealth generated by those mines might trickle down?

Well, as I was about to find out, it isn't. And it doesn't. So, like I say, you could hardly blame the border guards for treating a bunch of guys from the West with suspicion. Historically, it was blokes like us who came into their country, took what we wanted and left a God-awful mess in our wake.

During the first portion of our stay in the Congo we visited Panzi Hospital, run by the remarkable Dr Denis Mukwege. There I got to meet some of the victims of rape and sexual violence.

I knew the rapes in the Congo were brutal, but even so, nothing could have prepared me for what I was about to learn at the Panzi Hospital. Rape, I discovered, is being used as a weapon of war: soldiers force fathers to rape their own daughters and brothers to rape sisters. Dr Mukwege introduced me to women who had had their lower arms cut off from just above the elbow so they can never hold anything again, who had been repeatedly gang-raped, been penetrated with guns and knives, and had burning wood and molten plastic bottles pushed into them – that's how deep the hatred is.

And afterwards? The poor victims are ostracised. In many, if not most instances, they're carrying the babies of their tribe's most hated enemies, so they're rejected by their families, by other women. Everybody. In the eyes of Congolese society they've been defiled and they are, effectively, cast out.

That was very, very hard to understand. On top of the barbarity and inhumanity of the original act comes that next insult. The fact that women who have been victims of such terrible violence are then shunned by their own families defies belief.

Leaving the Panzi Hospital that day I did a piece to camera saying I wanted to look into the eyes of a man who was capable of doing this to another human being. And that, in the end, is what I did. (See R is for (the thankfully) Rare Glimpses of Evil.)

First we had to find them. Which meant a UN supply flight out of Goma to Walikale, a town some way from civilisation, where roads are in short supply but jungle is plentiful – jungle that hides thousands of Hutu militia men who wage a constant war against the UN peacekeepers, an Indian unit called the Fighting Fifth. It's their job to stop marauding militia attacking the villages and they mount regular patrols. How do normal people get around? The answer is they don't, unless the army escort them on the ground. No doubt about it, we were sticking close to these guys.

Strapping on backpacks and in my case a wide-brimmed hat, we joined members of the Fighting Fifth on patrol.

It was hot that day – really, really hot. My cameraman was Jonathan Young; the soundman a guy called Jon Gilbert. Jon, poor guy, was wearing a lot of kit, including a sound mixer strapped across his stomach. So with the mixer and whatever he had in the pack on his back, he was a long vehicle, about the length of your average Eddie Stobart.

During the patrol we reached a log that spanned a small ravine, with a river below it going to God knows where. Could have been crocodiles down there. All I knew was that I didn't want to drop down there, a fall of – what? – thirty foot into the water below. But poor old Jon couldn't even get his leg up on the log, and for a moment he simply stood there, wobbling, lifting his leg like an oversized Thunderbirds puppet, hoping to try and make it up on to the log.

Heavy bush to my right and left made it impossible for me to see either, but I steadied him, and helped him up on to the log.

'You're all right, mate. You're all right,' I lied, thinking nothing of the sort. Quite the opposite, in fact – that the poor lad only had to overbalance by a fraction or so and he was going to find out first hand whatever was or was not down below.

Now, picture the scene. Making their way across the log were the UN escorts with the blue helmets on. After them came Jon, the long-vehicle soundman, complete with boom. Behind him some bloke off *EastEnders*. Behind him, Jonathan the cameraman. Then, behind us, more UN soldiers, who were tutting and sounding pissed off that we were being so slow.

The UN guys were used to it, of course. The ones ahead of us scampered across with all the grace and speed of ballerinas. Us lot, on the other hand, beetled carefully forward, moving slowly but thinking we'd be OK as long as we didn't meet anything coming in the opposite direction.

And that went all right for a moment or so – until we met something else coming in the opposite direction. A group of village women, carrying pots and pans piled twenty-foot high. The Indian soldiers ahead of us danced right round them. They seemed to defy gravity, like they'd developed Spider-Man-like powers. Meanwhile we media luvvies jittered unsteadily to a halt only to get a barrage of fresh abuse from the Indian soldiers behind, and were forced to carry on. Jon, the long-vehicle soundman, craned his head back to give me worried eyes over his shoulder, and as we nervously approached the chattering villagers I promised him that I would help him survive this tricky log crossing.

Which I did, by saying, 'Left a bit, Jon. Right a bit, Jon.'

Maybe he had something a bit more supportive in mind, but it would have to do for the time being.

That was just one moment of what turned out to be a bit of a heart-in-mouth patrol. Next we encountered members of the Congolese army. Hard-faced blokes who were as tough as any guys I'd ever met, from their narrowed, suspicious eyes right down to . . . well, not quite the toes of their feet, because for some reason the preferred footwear of the Congolese militia man is the white Wellington boot. I kid you not. White Wellington boots. Little dainty things. They were everywhere. It helped to take my mind off the AK-47s and rocket-propelled grenades (RPGs) they carried, the Chinese grenades hanging off their belts, and the fact that despite wearing the uniform of the Congolese army, they were former militiamen, and thus, probably, rapists and murderers.

One of the things I've learnt about modern warfare is that contrary to what we've been led to believe by the media, it's not waged by remote control. No, wars are fought and won by the men on the ground. He who controls the ground wins the war. Vietnam's a perfect example of that. Afghanistan is a perfect example of that. In Afghanistan it's our air superiority that keeps the Taliban at bay but the Taliban is still there at the end of the day, and will be when we've left. If you're an invader you have a home to go back to, but if you're an inhabitant you've got nowhere else to go and you'll fight tooth and nail for your piece of land. That goes for the Taliban, just as it goes for the tribal divisions in the Congo. I was reminded of that as I stuck close to the UN guys and tried not to wither under the implacable stares of the militia men.

With the patrol over we returned to the base and I was glad to leave the jungle, looking forward to a night in the safety and comfort of the base.

Except it didn't turn out that way.

Now, if you watch the film what you hear is me saying this: 'Unfortunately the UN can't put us up at their base, and we're forced to find accommodation in town, which is basic to say the least. It has no electricity, food or running water. But during the night I discover it has plenty of bedbugs, mosquitoes and rats.'

And that's that. The film moves on to the following day.

It wasn't just bedbugs, mosquitoes and rats I had to worry about, though.

We'd been expecting to stay at the Indian UN base on a hill overlooking Walikale, but the UN guys had a sudden change of mind.

It wasn't that we were unwelcome, explained the commander pleasantly enough, just that we weren't permitted to stay. However, he continued, we were quite welcome to return and have curry with them on Friday night. Nice offer, you'd think, but this was very bad news. In the meantime we had no supplies. No food, no water, no mosquito nets, nothing.

Disgruntled and a little scared, we clambered into Mark I Land Rovers and were given a lift down the hill and into Walikale below. It was beginning to get dark, and by now we were thinking of our stomachs, too, so at the director's insistence we stopped at a couple of ramshackle stalls. Waving away a proffered fish that looked distinctly unappetising, we opted instead for cans of tuna and corned beef each. It's not like any of us were great fans of tuna or corned beef, just that that was all they had, and believe you me they charged us way over the odds for it too.

With that done, the Indian army drove us to what they said was the best guest house in town. Which meant it was the only guest house in town, the only one from which we might possibly emerge alive next morning.

It was located inside a compound, which, as it turned out, was guarded. Across the entrance was a dilapidated vehicle, and for a while there was a stand-off between the Fighting Fifth and some weed-smoking militia men hanging around outside.

As it turned out, the militia men seemed to back down. On the other hand, perhaps they were like the spiders enticing the flies. Into the trap we went, like the obedient insects that we were. The vehicle was there to protect the compound from attack, of course, but it was also going to stop us leaving, too. Second thoughts? Too late for them. With the Fighting Fifth waving goodbye from their departing Land Rovers we stood near to the entrance of the guest house, surveying the groups of ne'er-do-wells lounging around the doorway. Like those we'd seen on patrol earlier, they were carrying RPGs, hand grenades and AK-47s. Any chatter had died down to silence and in the air hung the distinctive sweet smell of ganja as they regarded us silently from behind heavy-lidded eyes.

We checked in – if handing a few dollars to an uninterested guy on reception was what you'd call checking in – then made for the 'bar area'. In fact, it was a courtyard, featuring a table under a covered section at the far end and plastic chairs around the outside. We collected bottles of revoltingly warm beer from the bar and took our seats on the chairs, feeling uncomfortable beneath the stares of the locals. On a television the movie *Black Hawk Down* was showing on a loop. In the distance we could hear the beating of drums. They were beating down the sun.

Yes, that's right. We were in a part of the world where they beat down the sun. Hungry, we used our knives to open the tins we'd bought from the ramshackle stall.

Dominic, the director, had managed to get hold of a half-bottle of whisky. Before you knew it, he'd dragged himself to his room where he was out for the count before his head hit the pillow – successfully made comatose by the alcohol. Tom had his iPod and was consequently insulated against everything that was about to happen.

The rest of us, meanwhile – me, Jonathan and Jon – had decided the bar was not a safe place to be. There was the small matter of being told 'white men not welcome'. That and the fact that the militia men seemed to be really enjoying *Black Hawk Down*. These were stoned, heavily armed guys, and they were watching a war film. Call it extreme caution, although I'll call it prudence if you don't mind, but we decided to leave them to it and get the first look at our rooms, which were located on the floor above the bar.

They were horrible.

The walls were two-ply. There was no lock on my door, which wasn't even a proper door. It was like a saloon door, with huge gaps top and bottom, through which you could see the tops of people's heads and their legs. I had a thin, blue mattress, on a rickety wooden bed (still sturdier than the roof itself). I had no sleeping bag but at least the guest house provided a mosquito net. Only trouble was, you had to fix it up yourself. From nowhere, cameraman Jonathan produced a hammer and began to hammer the net to the beams above my mattress. Bad idea. From over our heads came a deluge of bug corpses that had collected in the floorboards above, raining down on us like something straight out of *Raiders of the Lost*

Ark. Hundreds if not thousands of them. I was still finding these things in my clothes weeks later.

Recovering from the dead-bug attack, we stared at the result of Jonathan's labour. A mosquito net peppered with holes you could have driven a truck through. No, let's not exaggerate. Holes that birds could have flown through.

There wasn't much in it, but I had the worst room. I was thinking, 'I own the company and I've got the worst room. How does that work? I own the company. I should have the *best* fucking room.'

From downstairs I could hear the sound of *Black Hawk Down* accompanied by raucous cheering from the stoned militia men. Gradually it dawned on me what they were doing – they were cheering every time an American character got shot and died. I don't know if you've seen *Black Hawk Down,* but in it a lot of Americans get shot and die. Consequently, there was a lot of cheering coming from downstairs. It wasn't a *good* kind of cheering, either.

Upstairs, I was slathering myself in Deet in anticipation of being eaten alive by mosquitoes. I'd avoided the blue mattress so far, but even so I swear I could feel bedbug bites already, plus I'd already drunk most of my water by this point and was beginning to feel dehydrated.

I reached for the tin of overpriced tuna and my knife. Grappling in the dark, I found my head torch and went to work in earnest, prising open the tin of tuna with my knife, and as I sat there in my pants and head torch, I wondered why I'd ever left *EastEnders*. I found myself craving a warm dressing room, a nice egg sarnie and a cup of tea.

I held the open tin of tuna in front of the meagre light from my head torch and inspected what could only be described as a dried biscuit, like a communion wafer of tuna after someone had somehow sucked up all the juice inside the tin.

That was the least of my problems, though. Suddenly, I badly needed a piss. God knows why, I was that dehydrated, but I needed a piss. I couldn't face going to the toilet. There was the small matter of the guys downstairs, plus I'd already seen the state of the toilet and it was foul. Really, really bad. Believe you me, I've had the misfortune of using some fairly rotten toilets in my time, but this one took the shit-encrusted prize for the worst in all history. From a hole protruded a family of squeezed-off turds stuck up at right angles, as if they were growing in there, like evil brown triffids. But even if you could somehow close your mind to that, there was no way you could stomach the horrific stench.

There was no way I was chancing that.

Instead I tried to use my water bottle, a plastic bottle of Evian. But it filled too quickly and I wasn't nearly done so I rushed to the window, planning to finish off on to the dust below. The window was nailed down. Desperate now, I hobbled to a corner of the room where a section of floorboards slanted away, and I breathed a grateful sigh of relief as I finished my piss and hoped – no, prayed – that it would soak harmlessly into the wood below.

But it wasn't that kind of night. Instead my piss rained into the bar below. *Kemp Piss Down*. I realised my mistake at the same time as an enraged shout went up below and the next thing I knew footsteps were thundering up the stairs towards my room. There was screaming in the corridor outside, and I imagined assault rifles and machetes being brandished as I shouted back, 'Sorry. Sorry. Sorry.'

'TV hard man Ross Kemp' here.

I listened. My apologies seemed to have placated them and they withdrew back downstairs to the film as I breathed a huge sigh of relief and took a seat on the bed. Well, I say bed . . . the blue thing in the room masquerading as a mattress. I sat in my pants with my head torch on, clutching my Gerber knife and listening to the mosquitoes and the sounds of the film from downstairs. *Bang. Bang. 'Ha, ha, ha, ha!'* And I thought to myself, if I can just sleep, then things will be all right in the morning. If I can just make it through the night . . .

It was so hot – that close, stifling heat you get at night – and I was sweating buckets, conscious I was losing fluid and only had a fifth of a bottle of water to get me through the night. Settling on my blue mattress in the forlorn hope of getting some kip, I became aware of the noises around me: from the room next door, two guys snoring; from outside, the sounds of the jungle – crickets, monkeys whooping, the rustle of nocturnal creatures. I'd seen the bats they have out there and they're huge – the size of cats.

I began to doze.

In the next instant I jerked awake. There was a sound

– the unmistakeable sound of two men moving along the corridor and tapping on a door, saying, '*Où est le boeuf?*' And, '*Avez-vous le boeuf?*'

Despite my limited French I knew what they were after. The beef. The corned beef. They'd seen us with it in the courtyard earlier and now they'd come out of their room from down the corridor in search of it.

'*Où est le boeuf?*'

They were whispering. Don't ask me why they were whispering. There was a bit of giggling too. I suppose it went along with the whispering. Giggling and whispering like a pair of schoolgirls – a pair of drunk or stoned schoolgirls.

'*Où est le boeuf?*'

They came closer to my room. I got off the mattress and went to the door, just a thin piece of wood between me and the two beef-hunters.

'*Où est le boeuf?*'

They were outside now.

Tap-tap on the door.

'*Où est le boeuf?*'

'No *boeuf ici*,' I said, praying that I sounded more assertive than I felt.

There was a pause.

'*Avez-vous le boeuf?*'

'No,' I hissed back. 'I mean, *Non. Non boeuf. Pas de boeuf.*'

That French CSE was really coming in handy.

There was a pause and I relaxed slightly, allowing myself

to believe the message had got through. That they had finally accepted my room was a *boeuf*-free zone, and that they'd return to wherever they had come from, their own rooms or downstairs to enjoy war films on loop. Wherever. Frankly, I didn't care where they went, just as long as they left the immediate vicinity of my room.

Silence.

'*Où est le boeuf?*'

Ever seen *Apocalypse Now*? Colonel Kurtz losing it in the jungle? You might know that *Apocalypse Now* was based on a book by Joseph Conrad called *Heart of Darkness*, except that for the film version, Francis Ford Coppola moved the action to Vietnam from . . . guess where? That's right, the Congo.

And here I was, having my own Colonel Kurtz, *Heart of Darkness* moment. A desperate and unhinged man losing it in the jungle: I was starving hungry and dehydrated. I'd been bitten to pieces and itched all over. It was stinking hot. There was no air-conditioning, nothing, not even a rickety ceiling fan. Just men with guns downstairs, drinking – beer? I don't know what they were drinking. It could have been human blood for all I knew – but whatever it was they were drinking, and whatever they were smoking, it was making them scary-wild.

So I snatched up my knife, threw open the door to my room and charged out.

Outside stood two men in jeans and short-sleeved shirts. Confronted by a man in pants with a knife and a head torch they stopped and looked at each other then back at me and they backed away holding up their hands like, 'No harm meant, no problem,' and off they went.

I watched them retreat back down the corridor to the stairs, and only when they'd gone did I breathe a huge sigh of relief and let my knife-hand relax.

The following morning, I woke to the sound of drums beating up the sun. The crew were met by a strange-looking figure. Wide-eyed and still traumatised from the events of the previous evening, I'd barely slept. I was a man on the edge of sanity. Dehydrated. Bitten. Emotionally traumatised. Hungry.

'Have you seen what we've got for breakfast?' said Tom.

Set out in the courtyard was breakfast, which was being cooked on a skillet that resembled the upturned lid of a dustbin and upon which a porcupine and a monkey were being roasted.

Not 'porcupine meat' and 'monkey meat'. Oh no. This was 'a porcupine' and 'a monkey'.

All of a sudden it dawned on me exactly why the two guys last night had been so keen to get their hands on some *boeuf*. If all you've got to look forward to is porcupine and monkey then a tin of corned beef must seem like foie gras in comparison.

Still, we had a job to do. And we were going to do it. We'd made contact with a group called the Mayi-Mayi, and were due to meet them. This was a Congolese militia group set up to defend themselves against other militias. Prior to meeting them I was told they used child soldiers and were involved in rapes, so I was dubious about the venture to say the least, but they turned out to be accommodating and gracious hosts. Laid on for us at a nearby parade ground was a traditional African welcome (although they had a few tricks up their sleeve, see L is for Lost in Translation), and afterwards, I spoke to a group of Mayi-Mayi leaders, where I was told they are the enemy of the Hutu.

Next they told me something quite extraordinary. When the Mayi-Mayi was formed they called upon the spirits of their ancestors, who gave them the names of special herbs they could use to fight their enemies. Not only do the Mayi-Mayi believe that the herbs made them strong, but also that if they take a solution of herbs in water it makes them bullet-proof.

I put it to them that the Mayi-Mayi had been involved in rape and they denied it vehemently. 'The magic wouldn't work if we did,' they claimed.

It's an understatement to say that we were glad to leave Walikale. We *could not wait* to get on that Sikorsky. But I'll leave you with two thoughts to demonstrate just how volatile and unpredictable life is in the Congo. Firstly, one of the Russian loaders helping to board the Sikorsky that day went missing. Taken by locals or militia, maybe because he was wearing a bit of gold, who knows? But he simply disappeared.

The second thing is that not long after we left, members of the Mayi-Mayi were accused of joining up with Hutu militia, raiding a village and over a four-day period systematically gang-raping over 200 women and children.

Was it true? The same Mayi-Mayi whose leaders had assured me that they hated the Hutu and that they would never be involved in rape because it would stop the magic working? I wondered: had the magic stopped working?

B is for Be Careful Where You... Oops, Too Late

D oing what I do, if you can hear the squeak of highly polished boots on highly polished floors then it usually – if not always – means you're in a government building.

Sure enough in El Salvador in 2007, cameraman Andy Thompson and I found ourselves in a world of gleaming marble and glinting chrome as we went to interview a government official for an episode of *Gangs*. The building's guards wore what I can only describe as jodhpurs, tucked into boots that had been polished to an eye-watering gleam, and I was led up a flight of stairs for what turned out to be a fairly useless interview. Not only did the government official want to remain anonymous, but he wasn't keen on answering any of my questions. All in all, a waste of time.

Anyway, on the way out, Andy had an idea: why not get a shot of my crabby old shoes next to the official's shiny boots as we descended the stairs.

Good idea, I said, and of course the preening official was happy about that. So we tried to keep out of Andy's way as we began our descent of the stairs and he started to film.

Now, I have the utmost respect for cameramen. Whenever people ask me about the dangerous situations I end up in, I always big up the crew and in particular the poor old cameraman. It's a bit like that old Fred and Ginger quote: that whatever Fred was doing, Ginger was doing it backwards and in heels. Same here. Whatever I'm doing the cameraman is doing while holding a camera and staring into a viewfinder the size of a matchbox. Never was this more true than in El Salvador when Andy saw the opportunity to get a great shot of a girl walking towards the camera. She had about twelve crates of eggs balanced on her head and looked angelic. It would have been a great shot – but for the fact that as he stepped back he trod in a huge human turd, biggest curler I've ever seen. Urk.

His fault, of course. He should never have been wearing his flip flops – or 'Aussie working boots', as our Australian cameraman Steve Lidgerwood calls them.

Which reminds me of a time in Papua New Guinea, filming for the most recent series of *Extreme World*, when cameraman Jonathan Young – another fan of Aussie working boots – had a similar experience.

We were in our hotel one evening when we heard the unmistakeable sounds of a gunfight, accompanied by the frenzied barking of guard dogs. Grabbing our gear and rushing out – half-dressed – we realised that the gunshots had been coming from a garage forecourt nearby and the barking belonged to the guard dogs chained to the petrol pumps. Because the dogs had got so excited they'd crapped all over the forecourt – and I mean *all over it* – and as we arrived hoping to film, there was no way for Jonathan to avoid it. He stepped in more than one. Got it between his toes. Ugh. Filming at 4 a.m. in your pyjamas with dog shit stuck between your toes – now that truly is above and beyond the call of duty.

And while we're on the subject, I don't think I'll ever forget an incident during our visit to Pollsmoor Prison in Cape Town (see J is for John Mongrel). I met three transvestite prostitutes, Beyoncé (who modelled herself on the real thing), Sandy and Charmaine. They were three very funny girls, or boys depending on your point of view – so funny, in fact, that at one point Craig Matthew, the cameraman, laughed so hard his half-moon, gold-plated glasses fell off and went right into the toilet pan.

Guess what was in there? That's right, something that wouldn't flush. Poor old Craig did his best to get them out. He tried using a couple of pencils like tweezers, but it was no go – he ended up leaving them there.

So anyway, Andy – the same Andy who walked backwards into the turd – was doing this shot on the stairs as the director and I came down. The trouble was that Andy hadn't seen the glass panels clipped between the stair and the stair rail, and as he came back with the camera he knocked one – and he must have given it quite a knock because one of those little star-shaped holes appeared in the glass.

As we continued down the steps I could see the crack spreading – and spreading and spreading. I swear it was still making its way upstairs as we walked out of the door.

That was a sticky situation – plenty of apologies and offers to pay required to get out of that one – but fast-forward a number of years to 2010 when we were making *Ross Kemp in the Middle East*, and there was an even more serious Watch What You're Doing incident.

We were really lucky making that film, we had an amazing fixer. Often we can't name our fixers for one reason or another, mostly their own protection – and this is one such case – which makes them the unsung heroes of the films. This one, in particular, was beyond great, he was fantastic. How else could we have gained such incredible access to the Popular Resistance Committees (PRC) and Islamic Jihad? These were the guys who fired homemade missiles from the Strip into Israel and leave improvised explosive devices (IEDs) for Israeli troops. Getting the chance to meet them was a scoop. Nerve-racking, but still a scoop.

All the time we were in Gaza I was convinced we were being watched. Call it paranoia if you want but if it's all the same to you I'll call it a case of being sensibly cautious. Anyway, there were evidently other people who thought we were being watched, too. On the night we went to meet the members of the Popular Resistance Committees (PRC) a coalition of various armed Palestinian factions that oppose the conciliatory approach adopted by the Palestinian Authority and Fatah towards Israel and who specialise in planting road-side bombs and vehicle explosive charges, we left our hotel then had to swap vehicles three or four times before we got to the meeting location. Along for the ride were me, Tim Watts the soundman, Andy Thompson on camera, producer Tom, director Ollie Lambert and the fixer/translator.

And we were getting more and more nervous the more car-swapping we did, wondering what the hell was the point, because we were going to stand out however many times we changed cars. Next we were told to remove the batteries from our phones and Andy was ordered to switch off the camera. And then we waited – for over an hour we waited – until we were greeted by a contact and told to follow a white Jeep. On we went.

We arrived, in the end, at a house on a hill in Gaza where we were greeted by a man in black combat wear, wearing a black balaclava with Arabic writing on the front. We nodded our greetings and were led through a passageway into what at first glance looked like a kitchen.

And what, on second glance, proved to actually *be* a kitchen – or had been once. Only, instead of having pots and pans and Nigella Lawson standing around, it had missiles, dozens of them, lining the walls like nine irons in a golf-club shop, while in the sinks were mortars in various stages of construction.

In other words, there were an awful lot of explosives in the room.

There were a lot of PRC balaclava wearing, armed guys hanging around too. It didn't escape my notice that one of them was toting an M60, the big machine-gun, the one Rambo uses – one of those.

As ever, the leader was the smallest, most wiry guy in the room. The interview began and was a bit stilted and wary as he started to explain his ideology and I tried to put my paranoia to one side. Not only was I worried about something in the room going off, but there was also the danger of a possible Israeli attack. Casting my eye around the room, at the missiles in tubes leaning against the walls and the mortars in the sink, it struck me that I wasn't in a kitchen so much as in a target for Israeli intelligence – either a bomb from a drone or an F16.

A quick word about soundmen. Spare a thought for them. Me, I'm front of camera, I've got the glamour job. The cameraman? Everybody respects the cameraman because film is a visual medium so whatever the cameraman wants, the cameraman gets. Even the director gets to stand around and give orders.

But the soundman? He gets to stand there holding a boom, with everybody wondering why we don't just record the sound through the camera, like you do on your video camera at home.

Qualities needed to be a soundman? Well, apart from a good ear, an aptitude for sound and atmospherics, and plenty of patience, on a purely practical level, you'd have to say that being tall helps. You need to be able to hold the boom overhead. Plus, it's not a job for shrinking violets. A soundman has to get in there, shove people aside if necessary. Like I say, they'll all be making way for the camera, but we need sound, too, so he's got to be wherever the camera is to record it.

Tim was the soundman in the kitchen that night. As the PRC leader and I spoke he held the mic to catch every word we said. And he was very carefully moving the boom between us, which meant having to move back slightly . . .

What I heard – and this'll stay with me forever – was this sound: *tink*. Like the sound made by a fork on a wine glass the size of a fish bowl, the best man rising to give his speech.

The room froze as the *tink* was followed by a *clunk*, and our tiny, nervy minds tried to process what was happening. Was the door about to open to Mossad agents pouring in, assault rifles chattering as they sprayed the room? Or was the *tink* followed by a *clunk* the sound you hear immediately prior to a drone strike?

And then it became clear.

Clunk-clunk-clunk went the missiles. Tim the soundman had knocked one with his boom and it had set off a chain reaction. We watched dumbstruck as like dominos the missile tubes, each one stuffed with propellant and a highly volatile homemade warhead, toppled one after the other.

The guy holding the M60 – I swear his eyes actually bugged out of his balaclava as we all watched the missiles fall over until it came to the very last one, the one at the end of the line, which wobbled slightly, but remained upright.

There was a dreadful, shocked silence in the room as we all watched the last missile settle. We swallowed, each of us suddenly realising we'd been holding our breath. And then we looked at one another – and we burst out into hysterical laughter.

And after that? The interview was a breeze. Religion, politics, race aside, even Tim laughed after saying 'Sorry' about 200 times.

C is for Carrier-Bag Cavity Search

O uch. Something I've done plenty of over the years is drag my crew into various prisons, some of which have been easier to film in than others (see P is for a Prostitute Called Margarita). One particular episode that sticks in my mind was in El Salvador, filming for *Gangs*, when we spent some time with a bunch calling themselves the Little Psychopaths of Delgado City, members of MS-13, who lived on the outskirts of El Salvador's most notorious city. Initiation into MS-13 involves murdering a member of the opposing 18 Street gang, or being beaten for thirteen minutes. Piss off these guys in prison and legend has it they'll cut off your head and play football with it.

So on the one hand, yes, these were tough guys. Like the rest of the gangs in El Salvador they were always armed and, of course, heavily tattooed. Thanks to a gargantuan appetite for weed they also spent most of their time comatose, which was either a blessing or a curse, depending on which way you looked at it.

But on the other hand? They lived in grinding poverty in the barrios of San Salvador, with very few opportunities for escape, and they were scared. Not that they'd have admitted it, obviously. But they were. They lived in fear.

One of them was a guy named Chucho (see S is also for Soft Toys), and it was through him that we came to be visiting the El Salvador female prison. His wife Ingrid was in there, and while imprisoned she'd had Chucho's baby. Understandably, Chucho wanted to see his new little girl but getting to the prison was á problem for him. As a high-ranking MS-13 member, if he was spotted on public transport he'd either be arrested by the cops or killed by a rival gang member. There you have it: one of the pitfalls of being a known face in the gang world and not having a car. You're stuck.

In other words, this was a guy in need of a lift.

So we decided to set up a visit, help Chucho meet his little girl for the very first time and get some footage as well, and the responsibility for setting all of this up fell to our researcher, Marta Shaw.

A quick word about Marta. Great person. Very tough and one of the pathfinders for *Ross Kemp on Gangs*. A genuine heroine of the series and for that I thank her.

One person who won't be thanking her, however, is the poor fixer Marta engaged for the purposes of getting in and out of the prison, a bloke we'll call Rolando.

Being able to speak the lingo, Rolando was asked to go in and set up the visit, but it turned out to be quite an ordeal for him. He was cavity searched. The normal way of cavity searching someone is to use hygienic, disposable gloves and lubrication, but not these wardens, oh no. Whether it was a cost-cutting measure or they were unusually environmentally friendly, I don't know, but these guys used plastic carrier bags from the local supermarket.

Rolando was tough, so he came through the experience unscathed and with a somewhat queasy smile on his face. The rest of the crew – that was me, the director, Anthony, the soundman Tim Watts, and cameraman Andy Thompson – were a slightly softer lot, and we had a nervous week of waiting to find out if we were about to violated by carrier bags too.

'I'm sure it won't be that bad,' I told them, wishing I could believe it.

The day came and we entered the prison. Prisons have a very particular atmosphere – one you never really get used to. There's a constant noise that doesn't die down, and a smell – difficult to describe but really quite unpleasant, a mixture of shit, piss, BO, and detergent if you're lucky. It's the smell of people held in confinement, and it stays in your nostrils for a long time afterwards.

This prison was no different just because the inmates were women. In many ways, of course, they were a breed apart. The women of the El Salvador gangs had an unbelievably tough time of it. Rape was a feature of involvement with the gangs and the women would have a choice: rape by 'hurt', which is what it says on the tin, or rape by 'love', which involves less violence but includes lots of men 'running a train' on the poor girl, and a subsequent loss of respect afterwards. That right there is pretty much a definition of 'a rock and a hard place'.

Not only that, but female gang members would be expected to deal out as much violence as their male counterparts. During my fortnight in El Salvador I spoke to girls who were trying to leave the life and wore heavy make-up to disguise the tattoos. Lovely girls but their casual attitude to the murders they'd committed was pretty shocking stuff.

So we awaited our entrance into the prison. Nervously. Especially nervously because of the upcoming cavity search.

I can't remember how we decided who would go first, but let's say that I manfully volunteered for the task. Whatever – I walked into the room where two guys were waiting for me and without further ado, dropped my pants, thinking, *Might as well get it over with.*

The two warders looked at each other, then at me.

They looked at each other again, the expressions on their faces saying, *What is this mad gringo on?*

I stood there for a second with my pants and trousers around my ankles. They looked at me, then at each other, mouths open.

Until at last the penny dropped. There was to be no carrier-bag cavity search.

Thank the Lord. God knows what those two blokes thought of me, dropping my trousers and standing in front of them stark bollock naked but, breathing a sigh of relief, I hurriedly pulled up my trousers, gratefully accepted the wooden ID disc I was given and returned to the crew.

But of course, you're not going to pass up the perfect opportunity for a wind-up, are you? Oh no.

Entering the room I rearranged my features into an expression of ashen-faced trauma, walking gingerly, like a man who'd just had a carrier bag shoved up his back passage.

They looked at me and gulped.

'I think you're next, Andy,' I said, indicating the poor, stricken cameraman.

'I'm not doing it,' he quaked, 'you can't make me do this. I don't get paid enough for doing this.'

I gave him an encouraging clap on the back. 'Come on, mate, it's not that bad. It'll be over before you know it.'

Off he went, meek as a lamb.

Two minutes later.

'Kemp, you bastard!'

Once we'd collected ourselves we passed through to the prison, where we met up with Chucho, his mother and his wife, Ingrid. There we watched as Chucho made the acquaintance of his new baby daughter, and I witnessed the other side to some of the women incarcerated in the prison. The maternal side.

As for Chucho, well, I'd have to say I saw a different side to him as well – the new father and husband who was delighted to see his baby for the first time.

So delighted, in fact, that while the crew and I couldn't wait to get out of the prison, Chucho stayed the night.

D is for Don't Go Jumping Over People's Fences, Especially If You're in…

Belize. You'll find it on the map just below Mexico and to the right of Guatemala, and let me tell you, you have never seen such a beautiful place in your life. As well as stunning natural scenery inland it's one of the top diving spots in the world – maybe *the* top – and is home to the Great Blue Hole, a huge sinkhole on the east coast considered to be one of the world's most jaw-dropping sights.

As you can probably guess, however, I wasn't there for the diving.

No. I was there because Belize plays an essential part in a global cocaine trade worth over $23 billion a year. Over a third of the coke making the journey from production in South America to consumption in North America passes through there. Why? Because it's got dozens of small islands and mangroves, not to mention miles and miles of (virtually) unprotected coastline and (almost) unguarded land borders.

Of course, where you find drugs, you find crime and gangs, and Belize is no exception. Matter of fact, it's practically the world leader when it comes to crime and gangs. Great for diving it may be, but it's also a great place for getting shot, especially if you wander into some of the rougher areas of Belize City, the base for an incredible twenty-three gangs.

We were there to film an episode of *Gangs,* and had landed and got to our hotel.

Now, this hotel. I forget the name but I'm not sure they'd want the kind of publicity I'm about to give them so we'll leave it out anyway. It looked great on the outside, but once we got in we realised it had all the usual drawbacks, which in this case included exposed wiring and the fact that they'd left the windows open in the middle of a tropical storm. Above the bed was a fan, one of those lazy things that looks good in the movies but does sweet FA in real life. Thanks to the storm blasting through the open window it was lit up like a Christmas tree. Electricity was sparking off it and splashing to the floor. The bed, meanwhile, was awash. It was no longer a bed. It was a swimming pool.

'Oh my God,' I groaned, mentally saying farewell to any chance of a good night's kip. Also on the team was Tom Watson, one of the best producers on the planet, and what rubbed salt into my shit-room woe was knowing that whatever room he was in it would be the best one. Either because he's the researcher, has a knack for it or is just plain lucky, but Tom Watson *always* gets the best room (and in general, you have to say, he deserves it).

So anyway, we were staying in this hotel, and after a day's shooting we'd grab something to eat and a drink – all right, a *few* drinks, especially on the night in question – and make our way back to the hotel, a route that took us along the beachfront and past some really nice houses. Like everywhere you go in the world, Belize isn't a poor place if you're rich. It's only poor if you're poor. And the majority are.

There was one particular house we always passed, a little scruffier than the rest. We'd been told by more than one local that it belonged to a white man who dabbled in witchcraft. Not only would this guy put a spell on you if you messed with him, but they said he'd had a wife, and that he'd killed her, mummified her body and hung her on a hook in the house. They said that if you got close enough to the house and looked through the window you could see her desiccated corpse inside, her dead sightless eyes staring out at you.

One thing you should know about me: I don't judge. This is true personally as well as professionally. In everyday life, I hate the whole thing of being judged, people judging each other, et cetera, and when I'm making a film, something I always bear in mind is that there are two sides to every story. The guy in the Congo who's done terrible, inhuman things? The last thing I want to do is to excuse him, but you do well to bear in mind that he's probably had terrible, inhuman things done to him or those he loves – that he's part of a horrific cycle of violence in motion. So, because of a personal bugbear, not to mention professional ethics, I try not to judge. And that goes for everything, witchcraft included.

Only, I was a bit pissed, wasn't I? And I was thinking, 'Ghosts and ghoulies? Yeah, right.' And as we stood there, gazing at this supposedly haunted house, I found my gaze travelling up the seven-foot high security fence, the sort you get at basketball courts, and I thought to myself, 'I could make it over that.' (Alcohol – don't you just love it.)

The next thing you know, I was trying to do just that. I'd leapt up to the fence and was climbing it.

The fencing rattled. The crew behind me, which included our superstitious local fixer, were going nuts, screaming at me to get back down. They had different reasons, of course: the fixer thought I was going to be cursed for the rest of my natural born life; the crew thought I was going to do myself a mischief on the fence, especially seeing as it had lethal-looking coils of barbed wire running along the top.

I wasn't about to be told, though. A mixture of booze and bravado propelled me to the top of the fence where I negotiated the barbed wire and dropped the short distance to the neatly trimmed grass below.

It was dark, and I had to admit, despite the booze and bravado, quite spooky. Every area has its haunted house and as kids we'd broken into our local spooky home in Rainham in Essex, only to discover that it was just . . . well, an empty house. But there was a difference between a haunted house in Essex and a haunted house in Belize, where it was dark and where, even though it was hot, you suddenly felt a chill in the breeze that rolled off the sea.

And I started to wonder if maybe climbing that fence wasn't such a good idea after all.

Behind me the crew were urging me to get my arse back over the fence pronto, but nerves or not I'd come too far to back out now, so I ignored them and instead scooted across the lawn to the famous window. At the glass I stopped, steeled myself and peered inside . . .

They were right. The locals were right. In the dim lights of the room inside I could just about make out that there was indeed what looked like a woman who seemed to hang from a column inside the room. And she did look mummified. As my eyes adjusted properly, however, I realised what it was. I mean, what it *really* was. It was the carved figurehead from an old boat that the owner had kept for whatever reason. And it was unvarnished, which gave it that mummified look.

And that was it. Mystery solved. Eat your heart out Scooby Doo.

I was halfway through my sigh of relief when I heard a sound. The unmistakeable tip-tap of approaching paws, that kind of nylon-scratch sound they make on the patio. Attack dogs, you see, are silent – right up until the moment they pounce, and these guys were getting ready to do just that.

I've never moved so fast in my life. I covered the ground back to the fence in a time Usain Bolt would be proud of, literally launching myself at the fencing, which shook as I scrambled up with the shouts of the crew in my ears.

And if I'd managed the barbed wire a little gingerly on the way across I was much more reckless on the way back. I literally laid on it, swung my legs over my head and tumbled backwards off the top. Don't, repeat *don't*, try this at home.

D is also for Don't Be an Arsehole

O r D could also be for don't think you know best, or
don't be a clever fucker, or just 'duck'. It's doing what
the person on the ground tells you to do, whether that's a
fixer with local knowledge or the commander of a military
base. If the local person on the ground says duck, watch
me duck. When I was younger I thought I knew it all. In
the years since, I've learnt that I don't.

I'll tell you a story. When we were making the first
Afghanistan films we were embedded with troops in Camp
Bastion, which, although it's about the size of Reading
these days, wasn't too big at that point and you could run
the perimeter if you wanted.

So one morning a bunch of us go for a run: me, a couple
of members of the crew – who shall remain nameless for
reasons that will soon become apparent – and a few of
the men from the base. There were two rules: stick to the
perimeter and maintain the pace set by the instructor.

It was a decent-enough pace and I had no problem
sticking to it, but a couple of the crewmembers decided
they did have a problem with it and, perhaps because they

wanted to prove they were fitter than everybody else – wanted to show off, in other words – kept running off in front of the rest of the pack.

But they paid for it, twofold. Firstly, because the pace was set specifically to avoid getting a nose full of the caustic sand that is unique to Afghanistan – sand that's so sharp filaments of it actually cut your nostrils, and they both ended up with bleeding noses. And secondly because it took a lot of fast-talking to persuade the camp commander not to put them on the first plane home.

That's the golden rule. If you're being told something you're being told it for a bloody good reason. People who make the mistake of thinking they know better than the experts end up getting hurt or hurting other people or removed from the job permanently!

E is for Everything You Always Wanted to Know About Tear Gas Part I

Tear gas. A lot of people think it makes you cry, which, in a way, I suppose it does. But it's not like peeling an onion or welling up at the end of *Titanic*. What tear gas actually does is affect all the moisture points on your body. That includes the moisture in your eyes and in your throat and, if you're sweating, under your arms or on your crotch. And when it's activated, it burns.

Bearing all that in mind, imagine you have a terrible, sweaty hangover. Imagine also that the tear gas in question is the high-grade Israeli kind of tear gas, which burns harder and for longer than any other kind of tear gas I've come across.

Got it?

Right. What happened took place during the making of *Ross Kemp: Middle East*, a two-part film during which I spent time in the Gaza Strip, then went across to the State of Israel, the idea being to unravel what is one of the longest-running, fiercest and most complex conflicts of modern times, that between Jews and Arabs in Palestine.

One of the most controversial aspects of the war between the State of Israel and its Arab neighbours is the Israeli-built wall that stretches over 400 miles, separating the State of Israel from the Arabs of the West Bank. Israel calls it a security fence, but the Palestinians, along with some international agencies, have a very different view – they consider it a land grab. Nevertheless, despite the fact that in places the wall is in direct contravention of international law, there it stays.

A focal point for protests against the wall is the town of Ni'lin. From a vantage point on a hill overlooking the wall, protestors from Ni'lin hurl rocks at Israeli Defence Force troops to protest about the land grab, and the IDF troops respond in kind.

Well, not quite 'in kind', as we shall see. More 'with interest'.

Now, in the film, what you see is us arriving at the scene of this demo. What I don't mention in the film is what had happened in the hours beforehand.

And what had happened was this.

We'd filmed until two o'clock the previous morning with Israeli police in Jerusalem, where, I have to say, they were doing a sterling job keeping the peace in one of the most volatile cities in the world. After filming, we returned to our hotel, which was close to the beach on Tel Aviv. A secular city where the residents practise almost a live-and-let-live policy, Tel Aviv is a far cry from events taking place just a few miles away. It also has an amazing beach. Buzzing with residents and visitors doing beachy things in the day, it stays alive at night, when it turns into a nightlife hub. To our amazement and delight it was still jumping in the early hours of the morning when we returned from filming. Along the way we saw an open Guinness bar, and you know what it's like: 'Fancy a drink?' 'Be rude not to.' In we went.

Playing on the TV was a pre-recorded English football match and there was a fairly good atmosphere in the bar, and after a welcome first drink we decided to stay for one more, then a couple of whisky chasers – until, before you knew it, we were into a full-blown session. Put it this way, we were still there at eight o'clock the following morning, by which time we'd made plenty of new friends (and to give you an idea of how messy things had got, one of them was offering to cut my hair) and drank God knows how many pints of Guinness and whisky chasers.

But don't worry! We'd had a hard week; we'd we been in Gaza the week before and it had been really tough (see U is for Underground Tunnels), and we were relaxing, safe in the knowledge that we had a day off the following day.

Or so we thought.

We staggered back to the hotel just in time for breakfast, where I set about lining my stomach with the full Jewish ensemble: boiled eggs, pickled herring, cheese, everything – it all went down. And the whole time, as we were wolfing down this delicious breakfast, I was thinking of my bed, just a few floors above my head. How when I hit that bed I was going to sleep like a king. No, like a god. I hadn't slept properly for two weeks and not at all for about four nights so sitting there, still drunk and filling myself with breakfast, I fantasised about what was going to be by far the best sleep of my life.

With breakfast over, I bade a fond farewell to my drinking buddies and finally staggered upstairs to bed. By now it was nine o'clock in the morning, so I took a quick shower, towelled off, launched myself at the bed and was asleep before I made contact with the sheets.

And I slept. At last I slept.

And then was woken up. My phone was ringing. I grabbed for it and squinted at the time. Eleven o'clock. Eleven oh fucking clock. Tom was calling me at eleven o'clock.

I'm not particularly proud of this, but *mea culpa* and all that, I snatched up the phone, screamed, '*No!*' at him and cut him off, thinking, 'Fucking Tom at eleven oh fucking clock,' and jammed my head back into the pillow.

It rang again.

I ignored it.

But by then a little bell in my head had begun to ring. A bell that if it had a name would be called 'conscience'. And I had a terrible realisation. I knew this one thing. *I was going to have to get up.*

And sure enough, the next thing I knew, somebody was banging on the door. It was Tom, screaming, 'Ross, come on, mate, we've got to go. It's all kicking off. We're never going to get this chance again.'

It was Friday morning, wasn't it? It was all going off at Ni'lin and we needed to film it.

So, with a Herculean effort, I dragged myself out of bed. The combination of breakfast and a two-hour sleep meant I was no longer pissed at least, but I already had the beginnings of the world's worst hangover, the kind that had not quite arrived but like an advancing army you could see it just on the horizon and hear the noise it made.

I cursed my luck. I was supposed to wake up refreshed, that was the plan. Now I was going to have to suffer the full hangover in glorious Technicolor. As I heaved myself into my clothes I felt my stomach churn and lurch, a stew of undigested Guinness, pickled fish and eggs beginning to make its presence felt. If you've never been in this kind of state, then congratulations, and I really don't recommend trying it. But if you have, then you'll know what I'm talking about: when you suddenly become all too aware of what's sitting there inside you and when you start worrying that whatever's inside you might want to find its way out again.

We jumped in a Jeep and by the time we got to Ni'lin I was fully accustomed to the sensation of rising bile in my mouth and already sweating like a dyslexic on *Countdown*. For a moment, though, I forgot my hangover as we arrived to find a scene of open warfare. Good old professionalism kicked in. I dragged on my body armour and helmet, and we began filming.

On a bank on the other side of a wall ten or eleven feet high protesters had been hurling huge rocks over the fence to where the gathered IDF troops scurried into position. In war they say that whoever has the high ground has the advantage and you'd have to say that the Arabs had the advantage here. But they didn't have the firepower. Sure enough, just as we got there the Israeli commander was calling in a water cannon.

And not just any old sort of water cannon. This beast fires a green solution they call skunk. A mix of sewage, chemicals and animal manure, this stuff makes you sick if you come into contact with it, and it stinks. I mean it reeks to high heaven. No wonder the protestors withdrew as thick fountains of the stuff were propelled over the wall. Where we were standing was in the face of the wind and it was impossible to avoid the smell of it blowing back towards us. My stomach lurched. It's true that there's nothing like a bit of excitement to cure a hangover. Or at least make you forget it. It's also true that there's nothing like a strong whiff of chemicals, sewage and animal manure to make you remember it.

By this time, the crew and I had taken cover behind a blast wall, the idea being that we could film the protest from a position of relative safety away from the flying rocks. Trouble was, as so often happens, the protesters clocked us, and rather than being the observers we hoped to be, we suddenly found ourselves the target.

Having regrouped from the skunk attack, the guys on the other side of the wall changed direction, began scrambling along the bank towards our position behind the blast wall and started slinging rocks directly at us.

Now we were properly pinned down, and unable to move from behind the blast wall. It was an eight-foot high concrete wall with sight holes, but the Palestinians were using slings, the sort of thing David used against Goliath, and were so accurate with the rocks they were actually finding their way through the holes. Not all the time, obviously, but in addition to the rocks sailing over our heads.

We watched in dismay as Israelis crouched behind a blast wall not far away donned gas masks and began launching tear gas. There was the familiar *pop, pop, pop* as they discharged their assault rifles, firing smoke grenades over the wall. But it was pointless, because gusts of wind were catching the tear gas and blowing it right back at us. The protestors saw their chance, and with the wind in their favour were able to pick up the canisters of tear gas and start lobbing them back over the wall with the accuracy of Jocky Wilson.

The grenades trailed smoke as they came looping over the wall and clanged down by our feet, rolling and hissing as they dispensed gas.

Things were getting hairy now, the protesters proving as accurate with the tear gas grenades as they had been with the rocks. Every few seconds came the whizzing, firework sound of tear gas cylinders arcing through the air. Peeking around the wall was an increasingly dangerous activity, especially as we were being deliberately targeted by the protestors.

Pop, pop, pop. Whizz. Clang. Tear gas canisters were landing just the other side of our blast wall and by now smoke was everywhere, most of it on our side of the fence.

At one point I peeked around the wall, quickly withdrew

to safety then looked to my right to see Tom Watson, resplendent in a gas mask. Not only that, the cheeky sod was giving me the thumbs up.

Of course, muggins here couldn't wear a gas mask because I'm supposed to be doing pieces to camera, so every now and then the wind would deliver me a new gust of tear gas, right in the face.

Like I said, it affects any part of your body that's wet, which is why it's such agony if it gets in your eyes. If you're sweating – say if you've been up all night drinking, ho hum – it'll get you in any sweaty bits too. The feeling is like a constant stinging.

I tell you, I've had some bad hangovers in my time, but that one took the biscuit. My underarms were stinging and my sweaty bollocks were stinging, but they were like a mild irritation compared to my eyes. They were like two little globes of agony, like I wanted to pluck them out of my skull, and give them a good wash before popping them back in again. They stayed that way for the whole four hours – yes, four hours – we were pinned down behind the blast wall. God knows how I kept my breakfast down, but after a while I was glad of the sustenance, and once the sickness had subsided, it wasn't too bad – apart from the dehydration, the sting of the tear gas and the constant fear of being hit by flying rocks. The footage that eventually made it into the film is a compendium of about four hours of us being there.

And then, thanking God it was all over, and feeling absolutely snapped as they say in the army, we returned to the hotel.

There, I drank litre after litre of water. God, I don't think I've ever been so dehydrated in my life. Next on the agenda was to – *finally* – sleep, but first I needed a shower. I stripped off, climbed into the cubicle and delivered a huge sigh of relief as the warm water gushed over me.

A sigh of relief that turned into a scream of agony as the water re-activated the tear gas sticking to my previously dry skin. And suddenly it was as though I was being rubbed all over by a giant chilli, my entire body in agony as I crashed out of the shower, danced in pain around the room then set about desperately scraping the tear gas powder off my skin. I was red raw by the end of it, when I collapsed into bed, and, as I slipped into unconsciousness, I realised the entire thing had been witnessed by three old dears who'd been watching me through the window.

The next day I told the rest of the guys about the chilli shower, and it was Tom who said to me, 'You've been tear gassed before, Ross, shouldn't you have known better?'

'Yeah, it's all well and good when you have a gas mask, Tom.'

Anyway, this Israeli tear gas was some kind of superior-grade tear gas. I'd never known any tear gas have that kind of effect before. Secondly I'm never normally near a shower . . .

E is for Everything You Always Wanted to Know About Tear Gas Part II

At a railway station five miles outside Krakow in Poland, a city that is otherwise one of the most beautiful I've ever visited, nervous cops waited for a few hundred football supporters to arrive by train.

Not just any old football supporters, though. Arriving were fans of Lech Poznań, rivals of the local side, Wisła Kraków. And nor was it just any old train. For a start, the journey was five hours long, and because of the way fans behave, the train company gives them the worst carriages. Toilets? Forget about it. There was a hole in the floor. And when it eventually pulled into the station the fans, having endured this miserable five-hour journey in Poland's worst and oldest rolling stock, were met first by nervous riot police and dogs and then by rival Wisła fans baying for their blood.

The cops. Not just any old cops. Imagine the storm-troopers in *Star Wars*, except in black. That was these guys. Masked, heavily armed, many with rifles loaded with plastic bullets and some with canisters of tear gas strapped to their backs, and as the train trundled into the station, it

John Mongrel (an interesting guy).

All the gear, no idea.
45 Commando, Herrick 14.

One of the saddest things
I've ever witnessed – a glue
kid: a victim of inter-tribal
violence, Kenya.

Left: Dr. Mukwege. Proving that one good man is worth a thousand bad.

Below: Panzi Hospital – one of Dr. Mukwege's patients.

Opposite top: Johnathan Young films our interview with Satan.

Opposite bottom: Interview with Mayi-Mayi – allegedly impervious to AK-47 rounds.

Top Left: Child soldier, Congo.

Above: Me with Tom Odula, Kenya.

Left: My exclusive suite at the Walikale Hilton.

Funny how the camera lies – compound at Walikale Hilton.

Top left: Left to right: Dave Williams, Me, Steve Lidgerwood, Tom Watson, Southan Morris.

Top right: Welcome to the DRC.

Above: Left to right: Kiff McManus, Tom Watson, Will Churchill.

Haiti – looking back to where Tom got a face full of chlorine.

Port-au-Prince – a demonstration of how some of the buildings flatpack.

Suspects arrested by UN police in a dawn raid, Haiti.

The Haitian national
palace looking like a
wedding cake smashed
by a cricket bat.

The backstreets of
Goma with unidentified
crap. DRC.

Overleaf: All you can
eat breakfast at the
Walikale Hilton.

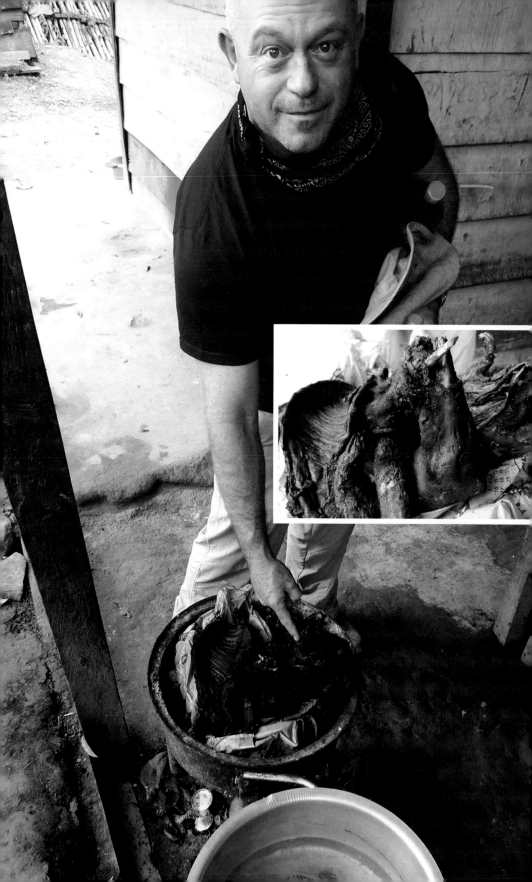

was as though an electric charge passed along their lines. They were ready for a fight – and in many ways were well up for it. These guys – not to mention the arriving Lech Poznań supporters and the Wisła fans who were waiting at the ground – were all anticipating the fight. I'm sure there were genuine fans who arrived inside that train, but looking at the guys who got off, 90 per cent of whom were shaven headed and some of whom were hiding their faces, either from the police cameras or from us, there weren't many of them.

The fans were herded on to a bus – you'd say 'like cattle', only cattle are treated better – then escorted to the ground.

Inside it was like a crucible of hate. All that seemed to separate the two sets of fans were flimsy, corrugated iron fences – at one point I thought they were going to come down, through sheer manpower. It was like watching a medieval battle.

Meanwhile, lines of riot police, still wired and up for a fight, roamed the top of the stands, ready to descend should trouble break out. What am I talking about: 'should'? There was no doubt – no doubt in anyone's mind – that trouble was going to break out here. Things had gone well at the train station: I'd been told that the fact the fans weren't chanting was a good sign, and that efforts to dampen their spirits with a dreadful train journey might have done the trick. But it was always going to be a false dawn because, let's face it, these guys hadn't come all the way from west-central Poland just to enjoy a great game of football and a bit of friendly banter with the Wisła fans.

Oh no. These guys were here for a fight. Pissed-up, hungry and freezing, but still up for a fight.

And they were going to get it.

About five minutes after the whistle was blown and the match started, something unusual caught my eye. One of the fans in the Wisła end, close to where I stood, was not presently involved with either chanting or yelling abuse at the visiting supporters. Instead he stood talking seriously into his mobile phone, his eyes fixed on a point over my shoulder. I swung around and looked to the other side of the ground, following his gaze. There, standing on the Lech Poznań terraces, was a corresponding phone user. He, too, was speaking into his phone, eyes fixed on his Wisła counterpart.

To me it was obvious: these guys were talking to one another. They were both laughing. Were they the ringleaders, bantering with a few choice insults ('whore' being a popular and particularly rude Polish insult)? Or were they organising the afternoon's entertainment, doing the football hooligan equivalent of setting a date for later? Not so much 'ladies who lunch' as 'lads who lump each other'.

Either way, whether the mobile phone conversation was part of it or not, it did indeed kick off.

It was the fans right in front of me, the Wisła crew, who started it. Unable to reach the Lech Poznań visitors they instead turned their attentions on the security and police. Rooted to my spot by the side of the pitch I felt the force of the violence come blasting off the stands as fans raced across the terraces and towards security guards.

With a roar the marauding fans charged a line of clear riot shields, attacking them with a clatter of boots on Perspex. In return the guards began pushing back, wielding rubber truncheons and clobbering the fans, who scrambled back ready for a second massed attack.

To try and prevent another charge the security guards deployed tear gas. Like I said, they carry it in canisters on their back, the kind of thing gardeners employ to carry weedkiller, except with a far greater range. This I found out to my cost when, thanks to a slight case of overgassing plus an unfortunate gust of wind, I caught a dose of it in the face.

And *wow*, that was painful. Like being repeatedly slapped across the face. Imagine, in fact, somebody is repeatedly slapping you across the face and you, for some reason, cannot move your face away. It stings. By God, it stings. It makes you cough and, as I've already described, your eyes well up until it feels like they're going to swell up and boil right there in your skull. And, of course, it gets you in your throat too. I mean, if you're standing there with your gob open as I obviously was, it'll get in your throat. You can even feel it in your ears.

To be honest, though, in the end, it wasn't the tear gas I was most worried about. As the violence continued to rage, with the fans charging the security guards, the baton-wielding guards charging back and the match having long since been suspended, what concerned me was that some of those rather lightweight-looking barriers might come down.

Thankfully they didn't. We emerged from the stadium unharmed, if a little shaken, and in my case with streaming eyes and stinging skin, wondering why on earth they call it the beautiful game.

East Timor was where I got my next dose of tear gas.

In 2002, when the Indonesians were told to leave East Timor thanks to a UN referendum, this tiny country lodged between Indonesia and Australia became the world's youngest democracy. However, it began an era of vicious infighting as rival factions within the country vied for power. It's in such conditions that gang culture flourishes. Sure enough, in East Timor it's said that a fifth of the population are gang members of some sort.

And that, of course, was why we had made it our destination for an episode in the second series of *Gangs*. While there, I witnessed strange initiation ceremonies, was introduced to some bizarre weapons the like of which I had never seen before, and saw some jaw-dropping martial arts in action. It was also my next experience with tear gas.

It really kicked off during our last day. We had just conducted what we thought would be our final interviews, including one with the president, José Ramos-Horta, and were getting ready to leave, little knowing that a major political situation was just about to come to the boil. Shortly after we'd spoken to him, Ramos-Horta had announced the name of his prime minister and the gangs supporting the losing candidate were none too happy about his decision. Trouble kicked off in the internally displaced persons (IDP) camp in the capital city Dili, which was across from our hotel. I've seen some pretty horrible IDP camps in my time: the Eldoret Showground in Kenya, home to countless displaced persons, stretched literally as far as the eye could see. And what I knew was that they're breeding grounds for disease, for criminality, for gang activity – the perfect place to go if you need to whip up political support of a violent disposition. If you wanted to start a riot, in other words.

The word came round that there was a disturbance at the IDP camp, so out we rushed.

The thing was, I wasn't long back from Afghanistan at this point. I'd been used to .762 rounds and RPGs whizzing over my head, so I wasn't worried about a few rocks. I should have been, of course, and must have had rocks in my head not to have been, but I can only tell you how I felt at the time, which was up for anything. It wasn't uncommon for me to go piling into some situation, doing what I thought was a piece to camera, only to turn around and discover there was no cameraman with me (some cameramen do wars; some don't, because some have seen too much).

This was one of those times. I had to run back and collect the cameraman as we rushed out of the hotel and across to the IDP camp. There we found the street already thronged with people, mainly gangs streaming from the camps who were throwing rocks at UN peacekeeping forces. And when I say rocks, I mean like huge boulders. The kind of rock that would easily cave in your skull if your skull got in the way.

We stuck close to the troops. Meanwhile, our fixer, Auricio, pulled me to one side. From a shop by the side of the road he'd grabbed a tub of cream and was slapping it in my face.

I reared back. 'Hey, hey, what the hell are you doing?'

'No, no, let me, it'll stop the tear gas,' he explained.

And he was absolutely right, because, as I've said, the tear gas works on contact with moisture, so what the cream does is set up a barrier between you and the chemicals that make tear gas sting your skin. Little tip for you there, if you ever find yourself in the firing line.

The other thing about the gas is that a lot depends on how it's deployed. And whether you're using grenades or even those garden-spray canisters the cops in Poland used, you stand a very good chance that a single brutal gust of wind will send the whole thing back in your direction.

Just as it had in the stadium at Krakow and the demonstration at Ni'lin, the weather played a part in the dispersal of tear gas used by the peacekeepers on the streets of East Timor. And once again, yours truly found himself with a face full of it.

But of all the occasions, I've got to say this one was probably the least painful. For that I have to thank Auricio – Auricio and some lady's cold cream or moisturiser, or whatever it was. Brilliant.

Still – it got my throat. There was no escaping that. Having taken shelter in a street that just hours before had been a normal street but was now filled with makeshift weapons that had been dropped in a hurry – bricks, boulders and sticks – and was thick with smoke from burning tyres, I saw an old woman, who was clearly in pain from the tear gas. She spat to try and clear her throat, and seeing her do it, I did the same.

Instantly she was glaring at me, then making her way across the street, a finger pointing as she jabbered something at me I couldn't possibly understand.

From the side of my mouth I said, 'What the hell is she saying, Auricio?'

Auricio, ever the lifesaver, was calming her down and in between speaking to her, told me, 'She thinks you're taking the piss out of her by spitting. I told you weren't. But she was about to stab you anyway.'

If you've seen the film you'll see I describe the East Timorians as a warrior race. There I had the solid proof.

Towards the evening, things quietened down and we retreated to a restaurant just outside Dili. Oh my God, these guys really know how to cater during a riot. The barbecue in this restaurant was at the table and we sat around eating great giant flakes of beautiful white fish. The restaurant overlooked the bay of Dili and for a while we were able to forget the violence still raging just minutes away.

Just then, Auricio burst in. 'Guys, guys, you better come right away. Your hotel is on fire.'

'Shut up,' we told him, 'sit down, have a beer.'

'No, no, I'm being serious. The hotel is on fire. Look.'

We piled to a balcony and looked across the bay towards the rest of the town. From the smoke billowing into the skyline it was clear that far from calming down things were only just heating up. Literally, heating up. Sure enough, one of the fires did seem to be emanating from our hotel.

Reluctantly we left the gorgeous baked whitefish (some of us more reluctant than others, naming no names) and tore across town, only to find that our hotel wasn't on fire – phew. Instead it was the building next door. A records office.

This is one thing I have learnt making the films: that when it all kicks off records offices are usually the first places to be burnt. That's often because it's in the interests of those behind the riots to destabilise whatever system is in place and how better to do that than by destroying official documents? In the case of the situation at East Timor, like a lot of tribal conflict, there are plenty of disputes over land and so . . . the land records go up.

Not that the records office was the only place alight. The whole city seemed to be burning. With gas cans in homes and buildings popping off it was an incredibly volatile situation. We reached the records office, which if anything burnt fiercer than many of the surrounding buildings. There we found an old guy throwing buckets of water on the blaze.

'Excuse me, mate,' I said to him, 'could we use your ladder to get some shots?'

(Yeah, I know.)

The guy looked at me, and his jaw dropped open in disbelief. 'Piss off,' he spat at me, 'just piss off.'

We moved on and ended up getting the shots we wanted elsewhere, but I could see his point.

What can I say? The excitement of the moment just gets the better of you sometimes . . .

F is for the Fine Art of Travelling Through the Peruvian Jungle Part I

If it ever seems as though I'm repeating myself during this book, then for that I apologise. But if it's worth saying once it's worth saying a thousand times: we don't judge. Wherever we encounter conflict, whether it's ideological or otherwise, we try to look at both sides of the story, let both camps have their say and allow the viewers to make up their minds. Never do we stand in the middle saying, 'This is wrong' or 'This is right'.

For that reason, with the odd exception, we don't get involved in the lives of those we talk to. We're there to report upon, not influence, events.

Even so, every now and then you have to stop, take a deep breath and remind yourself you're there as an observer, not as a normal bloke.

One such occasion was during the making of *Battle for the Amazon,* when we joined the police on a raid of an illegal gold-mining town deep in the Peruvian rainforest, called Le Mal (roughly translated as The Wrong). I was about to find out how wrong.

We'd got the access to this raid thanks to our fixer

on the job, a brilliant and brave man who, for reasons detailed elsewhere, must remain nameless. I think what he'd done was tell the police that we were in Peru making a film about the destruction of the rainforest, and that they might – just might – want to show the Peruvian authorities taking some kind of positive action to stop this destruction taking place.

Whether they had planned the raid without us or it was entirely for our benefit, I couldn't say. Fact was that after weeks of at times tense negotiations – and don't forget, there's always the risk that the authorities might simply decide they don't want to be bossed around by a group of gringos from England, come after us and nick all our equipment – we reached an agreement: we could join the cops and a prosecutor from the Madre de Dios area on a raid of Le Mal, the aim being to rescue underage prostitutes who worked there servicing the miners.

Getting there, though, was a story in itself.

The arrangement was that we'd meet the police at a secure point around ten miles from Le Mal. We drove for a day or so to get there, reached the meeting point in plenty of time and waited, but the time came and went, and four to five hours later we were still sitting by the side of the road, getting more and more agitated.

It's funny, because I can distinctly remember wishing I was able to enjoy this moment properly, thinking of when I worked on *EastEnders* when even though I loved being part of the show, I hated travelling, rushing around London for anything up to three hours each day, trying to make my way to the studios. And I can remember sitting on the edge of the jungle in Peru, wishing I could savour the total peace and tranquillity as the sun began to go down. And yet, I was unable to because of the worry that we might have been stood up by the police and the fear that we'd wasted a day driving to reach this point. It stopped me being able to enjoy the glorious surroundings. What if the police *had* simply decided that they didn't want to be bossed around by a bunch of gringos from England? 'We left them waiting for us on the edge of the jungle for forty-two days, ha ha! Big joke!'

Me and the crew have this thing, the knuckle thing. We'd seen gangsters do it, knock knuckles. But like a lot of piss-takey things you start, it had sort of ended up becoming real, something we did if we'd had a particularly successful day.

Good day today? Knuckles.

That day, though, as the hours wore on and there was still no sign of the police, nobody was doing knuckles any more. Instead, frantic phone calls were being made. The poor old fixer was in a bit of a panic.

And then, suddenly, as if from nowhere, came the roar of engines and from behind us trucks thundered along the road towards us, dimmed headlights sweeping across our position. And we knew it was on.

Scrambling to our feet, we watched as the trucks ground to a halt and highly armed Peruvian cops streamed off them, running to the tailgates and dropping them. In the next moment there was another roar as more cops on motorbikes came tearing off the back of the trucks. Assembled was a team, around fifty to sixty strong, some in uniform with bulletproof vests, others in plainclothes. Apart from the prosecutor there were some doctors and medical staff, whose function on the raid would soon become apparent.

There was no way of taking the trucks into the jungle. Either by accident or by design Le Mal was accessible only by dirt track, so the way of reaching it was by trail bike. We thought the police would take us on the back of their bikes, but there wasn't enough room. The idea was that a forward party – the heavily armed guys – would race on ahead to secure the brothels and hopefully stop any outbreaks of trouble while the rest of us would follow on. Follow, but on what? Our quick-thinking fixer saved the day yet again by legging it down to the road and hastily hiring four 50cc taxi bikes.

And then we set off.

As we began the journey it was starting to get dark and the cone of light from our motorbikes was hardly enough to illuminate the way. We came to a small, tented community selling water, biscuits and nuts. We were still in convoy by this point, trying to stay together, but then we continued, next stop Le Mal, and as the already narrow path became even narrower, the convoy began to break up.

The sky was burning ruby, blood-orange red through the gaps in the forest canopy. Getting really dark now. We were literally seeing stars appear before our very eyes. We hit a rope bridge, which a significant drop either side, at 50 mph. I gripped the pillion rails hard and clenched my teeth.

'Fucking hell!'

But if I was bricking it, then spare a thought for the cameraman, Will Churchill on this occasion. He was doing what I was doing, except he was looking into a camera at the same time. Kiff McManus, our sound guy, was holding on with one hand and holding the boom with the other.

On we went. Over more and more bridges, upwards of twenty of them, I'd say. A journey that took us the best part of an hour, and fair play to our drivers, these guys were skilled beyond belief. I couldn't have done what they were doing in broad daylight, let alone at night with a large chap sitting on the back, shouting in my ear.

What's more, this was the one route in and out of Le Mal, so as well as the motorcycles overtaking us, there were bikes coming in the opposite direction too. Just like in the Congo, these bridge users weren't bothering to stop, give way, or give a friendly nod and wave like a couple of Fiat-driving old ladies at a box junction. No, these guys came full pelt and sod you if you were in the way. Loads of times you'd find yourself brushing elbows with guys riding bikes in the opposite direction, knowing the slightest jolt might be enough to send you off-balance and plummeting off the side of a rope bridge.

And then, all of a sudden, the forest stopped. There was a clearing, another rope bridge and then the town: Le Mal.

I'd taken a helicopter over mining areas in the weeks prior to the raid, and from what I'd seen these temporary settlements were fairly small affairs, but this – this was huge. Le Mal was on a scale I hadn't dared to imagine, like a large town, a city. It appeared to be a cross between *Blade Runner* and a shanty town: a neon-lit, higgledy-piggledy, ramshackle place, a bit like a music festival after dark, with makeshift lights strung from the canopies of cobbled-together buildings. Among stalls selling fake designer watches, belts, T-shirts, you name it, were bars, many of them garishly lit 'video bars'. These were the brothels.

Though we were officially in the middle of a raid, the town wasn't in the state of uproar I'd imagined it would be, the advance party having quelled any possible disturbance. Cops with assault rifles had entered the brothels and were already beginning the process of inspecting the girls living there. Following the prosecutor, we entered the first of the brothels, only to be greeted by a foul stench of stale beer and mildew. The inside of these shacks were painted lurid, sleazy colours of luminous green and pink, and at the back was where the girls were kept. They cowered beneath plastic or tarpaulin, their knees drawn up to their chests, shivering and frightened. I stopped and had to resist putting my hand to my mouth, hardly able to believe they could be living in such terrible conditions. The smell of the rain, the plastic sheeting that most of the buildings were constructed out of, the mildew and the stench of stale beer stay with me to this day.

There were the usual cuddly toys (see S is for Soft Toys) and there were babies, too, being looked after by these terribly young mothers, none of whom looked eighteen.

Yet, of course, every single one of them claimed they were of legal age. This is where the Health Authority came in. Wearing surgical gloves, nurses inspected the teeth of the girls to make a ruling on their age. Most, it seemed, were around fourteen or fifteen, which figured. None of the girls were dressed particularly provocatively. Instead they wore shorts and vest tops. Not only were they underage but they wanted to look it. Why? The miners prefer sex with underage girls because they believe there's less risk of sexually transmitted diseases.

The police, of course, were here to 'rescue' them, but that in itself presented a dilemma. A lot of these girls, rescued or not, would never be able to return to a normal life. These were girls who'd been lured to Le Mal with the promise of a job in a restaurant or a bar. Well, they'd got a job in a bar, all right, just not what they expected. Having rescued them, the idea was to reunite them with their families, but many would be shunned or disowned, having been seen to have brought disgrace upon themselves or the family name.

To this day, I have no idea how many of them there were. As I said, this was a big town. There was bar after bar, brothel after brothel and the police, and Health Authorities were thorough, searching through each one.

One thing I was surprised about was the lack of resistance. There seemed no attempt at flight. Nor were the cops given any backchat by the girls. Yes, the cops were armed but even so: the girls seemed to accept this latest twist of fate meekly, accustomed to dealing with whatever life threw at them, I suppose.

We left the brothels, thankful to be back out in the night air away from the oppressive heat and stink and that revolting luminous paint, and I found myself standing nearby where some mineworkers were having a drink.

One thing I had learnt about the miners was that they have an odd belief. They believe that the more badly you behave, the more luck you accumulate. As a result, many were very abusive towards the girls. Physically and sexually abusive. And I became aware that three mineworkers were looking at me, laughing.

'Fuck you, fuck you, fuck you,' they were saying.

Just laughing at me: 'If it wasn't for all these police around . . .' kind of thing. Like it was all a big joke to them.

I wondered if these were the same guys who thought being bad brought you good luck.

I could feel myself rising to their bait, as I started to make my way over to them. Apparently, my non-judgemental self had decided to stay at home that night.

Tom stopped me. 'Come on, mate, let's go,' and I came to my senses in the nick of time. I did the right thing, the not-getting-involved thing. I walked away to the sound of their jeers at my back. Turning round and looking over my shoulder, giving them my best Grant Mitchell, I walked slap bang into a washing line of dripping wet knickers. Wet with what, to this day, I cannot say. Laughs all round from the miners, but better laughs than what might have happened if I hadn't walked away.

F is for the Fine Art of Travelling Through the Peruvian Jungle Part II

Prior to making these films, I'd never been what you'd call an eco-warrior. I love my car and the benefits that oil brings me. But at the same time I've seen close-up what our greed for the stuff is doing to the planet.

In Nigeria, an oil-rich country where one in five children dies before their fifth birthday, they burn the excess gases used in the extraction of crude oil, sending plumes of thick black smoke up to the atmosphere. Some of these burn-offs are ten buses high, six buses wide, an incredible waste of energy, and a constant source of light that affects the lives of people and animals for miles around. Seeing that burn-off at night for the first time was an eye-opener for me, and a major factor in what changed my mind about the environment.

Then, still in Nigeria – making *In Search of Pirates*, this was – there were the disused wellheads left by the oil companies and supposedly cleaned up (yeah, yeah) from which miscreants could help themselves to gallons and gallons of oil. Let me tell you, these guys are even less concerned about the welfare of the planet than the oil companies, and the mess they leave behind is unbelievable – a mess that often finds its way into the water table.

Another of those mind-changing moments took place in Peru while making the two films that became *Battle for the Amazon*. In the first film we'd visited Ecuador (see N is for Never Walk Around the Back of a Helicopter and T is for a Totemic Tropical Take-Off) where we discovered how the greed for oil has caused untold damage to humans, wildlife and forest. Moving on to Brazil we saw how beef production and soya plantations have destroyed acres of irreplaceable forest. And then, in the second film, we travelled to Peru.

Just as in Ecuador and Brazil, the wildlife and inhabitants of Peru suffer thanks to the production of commodities we crave in the West. It's oil in Ecuador. Beef and soya in Brazil. But in Peru it's cocaine and gold.

Fully one third of the world's cocaine comes from Peru. In the foothills of the Andes is the Vrae Valley, which, according to the United Nations, has more coca plants in it per hectare than anywhere else on the planet. There, makeshift cocaine labs are used to transform the naturally growing leaf into the base for cocaine. Every year around 750 tons of the stuff finds its way out of the Amazon basin and up the noses of pleasure-seeking Westerners, who fork out an estimated $85 billion on it.

And yet, despite the eye-watering amounts of money we're talking about, the Vrae Valley is one of the poorest regions in the whole of Peru. Illiteracy, malnutrition, unemployment – you name it, they have it. Not only that, but its habitat is being destroyed by its plentiful crop. It's estimated that 1,000 acres of forest are lost to cocaine production every day.

And yet, coca growing in Peru has been going on since the time of the Incas. And though a whopping 99 per cent of it goes into the illegal narcotics trade, it's still legal to grow a small amount for chewing or brewing in tea. You can see it on the market, right next to the papaya, bananas and limes.

Imagine for a moment that you're an ordinary Joe living in the Vrae Valley. The coca leaf grows naturally there, it's been cultivated for thousands of years, it's available at your local market and the chances are you know someone who makes a living, legally or illegally, from the coca leaf. In other words, one way or another you will almost certainly benefit from the coca leaf . . .

But on the other hand, the place is crawling with bandana-wearing paramilitaries whose job it is to stamp out the whole trade. They're trying to destroy your livelihood. It's fair to say that relations between ordinary civilians and the gun-wielding paramilitaries were frosty at best.

Into this mix add two white Toyota vans full of gringos heading for the Vrae Valley. Our plan was contact with coca growers there, see for ourselves what sort of conditions they worked in, and the damage the trade was doing to the environment.

First, though, we had to reach our base, a town in the foothills of the Andes called San Francisco. Same name as the one in California, but there the similarity ends. Neither should you be fooled by the word 'foothills', like we were right down at the bottom. Oh no. This is the Andes we're talking about. The foothills are in the clouds. Having arrived by plane, we began a ten- or eleven-hour journey at a fairly high altitude then clambered into the vans to begin a seven-hour journey to San Francisco, and believe you me, we were climbing every step of the way.

It was December. Rainy season. And the roads, which are narrow and badly maintained at the best of times, were partially flooded. Fast-flowing water streamed past us from the hills above, making the highways even more treacherous. But we climbed, and we climbed. Going was slow, and made slower by the fact that every now and then we'd have to stop and clamber out to manoeuvre the vans out of the mud. Then there were the bridges. A speciality in that part of Peru is the Very Rickety Wooden Bridge – a few planks of railway sleeper haphazardly laid between two banks. Luckily our driver was a Jedi when it came to negotiating them, while the rest of us became experts at staring out of the windows and shouting, 'Fucking hell!'

He got us across, though. Every time. You can keep your four-wheel drive. You'd see a hundred times more four-wheel-drive vehicles in Mayfair than you would in the foothills of the Andes. It's the skill of the drivers that keeps the motors running. They know the roads. They know the terrain. They know the people. To us gringos the sheeting rain looked like a daily dose of death and we approached each new obstacle thinking, 'What fresh hell is this?' But to the locals, it was just the time of year. No big deal. Nothing we can't handle.

And don't forget, we *were* gringos. On the roads a kind of community spirit reigned, and at times we were given help to push the van out of a tight spot. On other occasions, however, faces turned away from us, people spat, and one time, as we crossed yet another bridge, a teenage lad who was sitting by the side of the road raised his hand at me, his fingers in the shape of a gun.

A kid having a bit of a laugh at my expense? Maybe. But somehow, I didn't think so. I think he was saying, 'You're not welcome here.'

Still we climbed. We negotiated the Dragons' Dens – areas where locals would place stones in the road and passers-by would have to pay a small toll to pass. Still the rain came down. We were white-knuckling it now. We watched water seep in the doorsills and prayed the engine would stay dry – or, at least, dry enough to keep turning over. Torrents of rain fell. Every now and then we'd see a car literally float past us, swept away by the flood. Passing us going downhill was a constant procession of locals: in cars, on motorcycles, on foot. We'd see buses, rammed with passengers, not to mention livestock, squawking chickens and squealing pigs, like something out of *Romancing the Stone*.

Next we came to an especially steep section where a lorry was having trouble crossing a makeshift bridge, and having previously benefited from help out of a sticky spot, we jumped out of our own vehicle to lend a hand.

Around us was a tailback, perhaps a mile and a half in both directions, as we worked to try and strengthen the weather-beaten bridge – enough for the lorry to cross.

Water was rushing down from the hillside, a deluge of it that battered the lorry as we worked to thrust rocks beneath the wheels – anything to give the tyres a bit of traction as the vehicle progressed in tiny increments across the bridge, with nothing either side apart from cloud and the rush of water. There was not an inch, not a centimetre to spare. One slip, a simple weight shift, and the lorry would have plummeted from the side of the bridge and down the hill into . . .

What? We couldn't see, because by now we were above the cloud. Way, way above the cloud. So when you looked down what you saw was the lush green carpet of the treetops then the misty, dreamlike billows of the cloud cover. From our vantage point it was impossible to gauge how high we were. We might as well have been floating in space. When we breathed the air was thin, as though we were breathing in cloud vapour. Everything about our location added to a sense of otherworldliness.

At last we reached a summit of sorts then began to descend the other side. This time we were moving with the flow of the water flooding from the high lands, making the going slightly easier. We stopped to eat potatoes. Not like the sort of potato we're used to from the supermarkets at home, but some kind of weird discovered-by-Sir-Walter-Raleigh potatoes that to this day I can't decide were the best or worst potatoes I've ever tasted.

Not that we had time to savour them. It was only the briefest of pit stops to refuel, because night was beginning to fall and we were increasingly aware that we were tempting prey for the bandits we'd been told roamed the road – bandits who would place rocks across the road and make you pay to pass.

Feeling our bodies change as the air pressure dropped we came down into the Vrae Valley. If we needed any proof that we were entering Peru's biggest drug-producing area, where about a third of the country's coca is cultivated, then here it was: a traffic jam, with hard-faced government troops stopping and searching vehicles, and Jeeps by the side of the road, with troops on roof tops manning mounted machine guns. They were looking for drugs, or for paraffin, which is used to process the coca leaf. Eyed suspiciously by the troops we got through the checkpoint, and then we were in the Vrae Valley. After that we drove for six or seven hours to get to our final destination then – *finally* – we arrived. We were in San Francisco.

Built on the banks of a fast-flowing, surging river, San Francisco is about the size of a provincial town in the UK. One thing was for sure, though, we stuck out like a sore thumb. Here we were . . . well, perhaps 'the enemy' might be putting it a bit too strongly, but certainly we were viewed with suspicion. To the locals, white guys like us represented law enforcement or DEA. Like I say, the inhabitants of that part of the world have an ambivalent relationship with the coca leaf. The army guys, at least their intentions were obvious. But us? What were we doing there? What did we want in the Vrae Valley? We'd been viewed with suspicion by the troops at the entrance to the valley, and we'd go on to be viewed with suspicion by the residents of San Francisco. There's a lot of paranoia in that part of the world (not surprising, really). We really were out on a limb here.

For the whole time we'd driven, we'd hardly stopped, pausing only to eat and give the drivers a quick rest and a piss. For most of us, it wasn't a problem. All we had to do was stare out of the windows and gawk at the incredible scenery and grab a kip every now and then. And since this was in my loud snoring days I suppose I deserved it that they recorded me. For the drivers, however, it *was* a problem, and by now they were really flagging, absolutely knackered.

I remember I was just dozing when someone dug me in the ribs and told me we were just entering San Francisco. Opening bleary eyes I gazed out of the window to look upon what was to be our new base.

It was almost dark by now and I became aware of music playing somewhere. We began collecting ourselves, wondering aloud what the rooms would be like (not expecting much), while the fact that San Francisco was supposedly under the control of Shining Path was a topic of conversation, too.

A Peruvian 'Maoist guerrilla insurgent organisation', Shining Path was noted for its violent treatment of its enemies, be they the average Joe or elected officials. For that they had been given 'terrorist organisation' status by the US, the EU and Canada. As far as we were concerned, we could have been passing over – over to the Dark Side.

I became aware of music coming from somewhere, not Spanish, a kind of Latin music, different to any I'd heard before. Then I became aware of flashing lights at a building to our left and it suddenly struck me that there was some sort of celebration taking place.

And then, almost from nowhere, came this child.

It was a wedding, and the kid shot from out of the building where the reception was being held – right in front of our van.

We were only travelling at about ten miles an hour but even so, it felt inevitable that we would hit the boy, and I found myself with my hands over my eyes, expecting the bump.

Instead what happened was that because the mud in the street was so thick – like chocolate mousse – the van had been pushing this huge wedge of it ahead of us and, thank God, the kid was cushioned by it. He actually surfed it, across the front of the van, one of the luckiest escapes I've ever witnessed.

We shuddered to a halt. The kid, lucky though he had been, had made contact with the van, and as we piled out of the van to make sure he was OK, concerned adults began pouring out of the wedding-reception building to our left.

They were speaking a local dialect we didn't understand, but thank God for the fixer. He was able to calm things down, apologise on our behalf and then smooth things over when we took the young boy to a nearby hospital and made sure he was given the all clear.

That was a close shave. And that, after our epic journey,

was our welcome to San Francisco.

Little did we know then, of course, but that was about as good as it was going to get for us in San Francisco.

To be continued in . . . H is for How to Get the Hell Out of Peru in a Hurry.

G is for a Good Day at the Office

I'm lucky. Why? Because a lot of documentary makers are forced to decide on the script before they reach their destination. They arrive, doggedly follow what's on the page and then, whatever the circumstances, whatever situations greet them, make sure they get what they came to get.

We're not like that. Sky allows me time, and time is money. Conscious that a story can and will change – and that often the best films are made by taking those changes into account – we pursue not what we think the story is going to be in meetings back home in London, but what the story turns out to be when we're actually on the ground. It's that, plus a willingness (or should I say eagerness) to get our hands dirty, as well as a refusal to judge, that makes us different.

For those policies in action, you need look no further than the episode of *Gangs* set in Kenya. The film ended up being nominated for a BAFTA and though it didn't win, I think it got the nod for a number of reasons: firstly, because we were in the right place at the right time – or the wrong place at the wrong time – and were able to get the very best story we could, secondly, because we responded to what was a changing story, and thirdly because of what we achieved in doing something to help.

Planning the story back in London we intended to focus on Kenya's notorious Mungiki tribe. Members of this tribe, we learnt, controlled the Nairobi slums, and stories were rife of the decapitation and dismemberment of those who defied them. Cross the Mungiki, it was rumoured, and they wouldn't just put a bullet in your head, they'd cut you up, skin you, and leave bits of you all over the slum for all to see. Doing this was even more horrible than it sounds, because many Kenyans believe that if you're not buried whole then your soul can't pass into the afterlife. For the Mungiki the butchery wasn't just a way of striking a physical terror into the hearts of their victims, but a spiritual one as well.

So, a bad lot by all accounts. But arriving in Nairobi it became apparent that even those who opposed the Mungiki had to admit that their rule of the slums had had some benefits. They had managed to provide electricity, for example; they had put a stop to the roving criminal gangs terrorising innocent people. And when you considered that there were millions of normal Kenyans who considered themselves Mungiki supporters it was clear that there was more to the situation than met the eye.

In the days that followed my initial visit to Nairobi's Mathari slum, I found myself in a slum in a different part of the city; this one, Kayole, where I witnessed the police dealing with what they said was a Mungiki uprising. What I saw left me in no doubt that the police were a heavy-handed bunch at best, and I began to feel that things weren't quite as cut and dried as they first appeared. Well, they rarely are, of course. But in this case, even less cut and dried than what we saw at first.

Shortly after that, I accepted an invitation to meet three of the tribe's leaders. The meeting was to be held at the deserted home of Maina Njenga, the then-imprisoned leader of the Mungiki. The mythology of Njenga hangs like a shadow over the Mungiki, providing the basis for the fear that surrounds them, but also the respect. Legend had it that Njenga had died but upon resurrection seen a vision of how to lead his people, and so the Mungiki – or 'multitude' – was born. His stated intention was that the Mungiki should offer hope to those who have none.

I'm not afraid to admit I felt nervous just going to his house, unsure what to expect, and had no idea what kind of reception we'd be given by the tribal leaders who ruled in Njenga's absence.

We found it deserted, and open as we'd been told it would be. We'd been asked to go inside and wait, and so, feeling like dumb teenagers in a horror movie, we let ourselves in.

Sure enough, it was just as eerie on the inside as it looked on the outside. Looking around we saw a room dominated by a strange mosaic crammed with symbolism representing different religions: Christian crosses, Arabic crescent moons and tribal scrawls. The Mungiki, like most tribes, had religious roots, but seemed to have taken elements of their ideology from a series of different faiths. I was debating whether to simply jump in the car and retreat to neutral territory, when at last came the sound of people arriving. We listened to the crunch of tyre on the driveway outside then tensed as three men, their wives, and a fourth woman entered the mosaic room.

The women were dressed in the colourful robes you see on the more well-to-do women in Kenyan society; the men, meanwhile, wore suits, but not sharply tailored gangster-type suits – the kind of unassuming suits you'd see an accountancy trainee wear when trying to make a good impression.

It would turn out that the fourth woman was Maina Njenga's wife, Virginia (who as it turned out, only had days to live before she was tortured, raped and killed; her body dumped by the Tanzanian border). She, along with the other women, remained in the background as the three Mungiki leaders stepped forward to speak.

And you know what? They were a bit scary and intense, and I wasn't sure I believed everything they told me – for example, how the taxes they imposed on the slums weren't actually 'taxes' but a case of everybody working together for the common good – and I wasn't sure that they'd brought as much hope to the slum dwellers as they said they had. 'Hope', after all, is a bit of a subjective term – you might 'hope' you don't get your head cut off.

But there was also a sincerity about them. These were not the usual gang members I spoke to, who posed and preened and brandished weapons and on the one hand played the hard man while on the other claiming to be the poor victims. There was a bit of that, I suppose – the Mungiki were certainly keen to impress upon me that what I'd heard about the tribe was mere government propaganda – but otherwise, they were different, and I had to admit, I came away partially convinced by these guys.

It was a feeling that only intensified a few days later when, at the invitation of Steven, one of the Mungiki leaders, I took a trip to Dandora.

Dandora is what they call a high-density slum. Because it's also home to Nairobi's main dumping ground, not to mention the sewage works, it had earned the accolade of being one of the most toxic sites on earth. Having been there, I can only say it's an award that is richly deserved. I had a pair of Magnum boots that I could never wear again because the soles had melted due to the toxicity of the dump – and if it was doing that to boots, then what was it doing to people's feet?

I went to the refuse site, the workplace for thousands of slum dwellers. Competing with other scavengers, the rats and birds, they collect recyclable plastic worth ten shillings per kilo to earn an average of 50p a day. For a while, however, the poor, malnourished dump workers were easy prey for criminal gangs, who would simply steal their hard-won earnings.

According to Steven, the Mungiki put a stop to all that. You remember *The A-Team*? That was how Steven wanted me to see the Mungiki. And, again, I couldn't help but feel there was something in it. Perhaps they'd stopped the gangs by cutting off the genitalia of the leaders – a common Mungiki trick, apparently. Or maybe they simply had a quiet word. Who knows? The fact was they'd done it.

Then again, while a number of those I spoke to were keen to talk about the positive impact of the Mungiki, there were others who were too scared to speak to me, including an old woman who said simply, 'They will kill me if I do.' And I was left in no doubt that the Mungiki's main method of persuasion was the machete, rather than the messages of hope and community they wanted me to think. But even so, it couldn't be denied that although Dandora was by any standards a hellhole, it was less of a hellhole than it had been before the Mungiki got involved.

So you can see what I mean. The entire time we were chasing that story our perceptions of it were shifting. And rather than single-mindedly pursue the narrative we'd intended to cover, we allowed the film to change and (in my opinion) become a better film.

There *were* no answers as it turned out. But again, we're not afraid to say, 'We don't know, we don't have all the answers,' and know it's nothing to be ashamed about. After all, how can people from the West know how to solve problems that are generations old? Problems that include religious, tribal and political differences that have seen the shedding of so much blood over the years? Answer: we can't, and it's condescending to think otherwise. Not everything is painted in convenient shades of black and white. There are two sides to every story. Sometimes more. And sometimes the more you uncover, the less you understand.

It was during the making of the Kenyan film that I visited the Eldoret Showground. This was an internally displaced persons camp, an ocean of tents as far as the eye could see providing shelter – 'home' would be pushing it – for around 300,000 people. This was a prime recruiting territory for the Mungiki, I was told, and I could see why. Whether their intentions were malignant or benign or somewhere in between, the fact was that the poor of Kenya were drawn towards the Mungiki, maybe because there was simply no alternative.

However, it was while I was in Eldoret that I became aware of a place on the outskirts. A dump like that in Dandora, but lacking even that tip's basic infrastructure. It was home – and again I use that word advisedly – to thousands of what they called 'glue kids'.

Now, you've heard about glue sniffing, no doubt. There was quite a scare about it in the UK in the 1970s. It is, basically, the inhalation of solvents to get high.

Here on the Eldoret rubbish tip were piles of rubbish rotting in the forty-degree heat, a stench so strong you could taste it, birds that circled overhead and fought for scraps of food with the children who lived feral among the waste. And the unbelievable stink of glue. The chemical smell of it had mixed with the stench of the dump to create something that hardly seemed possible: something even more fetid, something even more toxic than Dandora.

Most of these kids were addicted to solvents. They inhale

it from little plastic bottles, breathing it in. I saw them everywhere, wading barefoot through the reeking rubbish with plastic bottles of glue hanging out their mouths, as casual as a Parisian with a cig. Others, in the throes of a more advanced high, simply lay almost comatose in the piles of waste, bottle gripped tightly – because however out of it they were they never lost their grip on the bottle. Jesus, it was horrible.

I saw them passing the bottles around, using sticks to agitate the solvent, get the vapours going, then inhale them, children as young as five or six.

And it was heart-breaking, like a living hell here on earth, and almost inconceivable to a pampered Westerner such as myself that these kind of living conditions could exist anywhere in the world; that any human being should have to endure this as life. Because I can tell you this much, it wasn't life. Not like any kind of life I'd been used to. It was *existence*, that's what it was. One short step away from death.

Mainly, they are the children of massacre victims. They're using glue to blot out some truly horrific memories, and yet by being hooked on it they open themselves up to rape and abuse. It really is a vicious, vicious circle.

They squat around small fires dressed in rags, or lounge on mini mountains of perishing waste. Fights break out often as kids squabble over solvents. The glue they sniff is used for shoe repairs. Occasionally they'll leave the dump to beg for money in order to buy more. And needless to say, it's killing them. The glue scars the lungs, which fill with fluid. The classic sign of a user is their wet wheezy cough. Plenty die from pneumonia and very, very few escape. The life expectancy of these kids is around sixteen years old.

Even so, they had the same hopes and desires as any other kid. They wanted to get off the glue. They wanted to go to school. The trouble is that in Kenya you can't attend school without a uniform (yes, I know; don't get me started) and where on earth were these kids going to get the money to buy a school uniform?

'I used to feel jealous when I saw other kids enjoying themselves,' said one, 'but now I realise that's just how life is.'

There was one image, though, that really seared itself on to our minds. Perhaps the image that made us decide to get involved.

My cameraman was Will Churchill, a brilliant guy and a great cameraman, the kind of guy who'll see things other people don't, who's always aware of what's going on and how important it is to the film.

As a result, he hardly needed prompting when I nudged him, pointing over to where a woman was gingerly making her way across the dump. Gingerly, not because she was holding a baby, although she was, but because she was so out of it on glue. She was a young mother, probably in her late teens or early twenties, though she looked closer to forty. Christ, a rubbish dump is no place to *take* a baby, let alone bring up a baby.

As she walked unsteadily across the uneven terrain of the dump she stumbled and fell and dropped her crying baby, which landed on its head. My first impulse was to assist, but as I began to make my way over she pulled herself to her feet, swaying slightly. And like many a mother she tried to pacify her wailing baby by putting a bottle to its mouth. Only this wasn't a bottle of milk, it was a bottle of glue.

You can't help everybody. During the making of these films we've met people in the very depths of poverty, victims of unimaginable violence. But other than telling their story and doing what I can to give them a voice, we've never been able to offer substantial material help. That weighs on you sometimes.

Tom Watson, Tom Odula, Will on camera, Kiff McManus on sound – we were all really, really affected by what we'd seen. The next day, Tom Watson went back to the dump in order to get releases (everybody we film has to sign a release giving their permission for us to broadcast the footage) and when he returned, he and I took a walk and found ourselves discussing what we'd seen. The kids, that mother giving her baby glue: neither of us could let it go, and we were gripped with the urge to help, to do something a bit more far-reaching than handing out spare change to a few kids, which would only be used to buy glue anyway.

The following day Tom looked for charities working in in that field. In particular Save the Children and a charity called Ex-Street – the latter, in particular, having especially good ties and contacts with the kids on the dump. The week after our Kenya special was broadcast we went out with a special half-hour film highlighting the plight of the glue kids and urging viewers to help if they could, ending with an appeal for donations.

The response was phenomenal, raising £250,000, and although I don't fool myself that anything has changed, I know that we helped reunite kids with members of their extended families, as well as buying uniforms to get them into school. We gave some of them an escape route – I can only pray as many as possible took advantage of it.

So yes, maybe we did help. Just a little. And that was a good day at the office.

H is for How to Get the Hell Out Of Peru in a Hurry

(. . . continued from F is for the Fine Art of Travelling Through the Peruvian Jungle Part II)

So there we were, in San Francisco. We found our rooms, which were basic to say the least, and – although not necessarily in that order – we located the nearest fried chicken place, where we'd end up eating for the next two weeks.

Next job? To make friends with the locals.

OK, I'm being slightly flippant here, because what became abundantly obvious, almost from the second we drove into town – and I think this would have been the case whether we'd had that incident with the mud-surfing kid or not – was that we were being treated with extreme suspicion by the locals.

What you have to understand about San Francisco is that one way or another it's a town supported mainly by the production of the coca leaf. However, we were there to make a film about how the cocaine trade is destroying the rainforest. These guys have monuments celebrating the coca leaf in the centre of town, then we arrive saying that production of the coca leaf is bad. Conflict of interest alert.

So not for the first time, we were way out on a limb here, and very much relying on the locals in our party, the fixer and especially one of the drivers, who was a San Francisco native. And, of course, the army.

How this rather shaky set of allegiances developed would come to be very important to our safety and well-being during our stay in San Francisco.

As I've said, it was the wet season in Peru and for San Francisco that meant not only was the high river fast-flowing and the roads, even in the centre of town, little better than mud tracks, but it was always, *always* wet. A constant moisture. It was in the air, in the clouds. At home, when you gaze up to the clouds they look pretty and fluffy, like little bits of airborne art to cheer you up on a summer's day, but they're not like that in Peru. They're just as beautiful, of course, but they're darker and seem to pulsate with the weight of the moisture within. The atmosphere is so hot and close that everything is wet, all of the time. So each day we'd leave the hotel in the morning and return at night, absolutely soaking.

And what I did each night was something that would come back to haunt me. I stripped off my soaking-wet clothes and tossed them in a corner of the room. After a week, it was a medium-sized pile of mouldering wet T-shirts, boxers etc. After two weeks it was a larger-sized pile of mouldering wet T-shirts, boxers etc. Like I say, I'd have cause to regret that.

For the time being, however, we went to work, and work was finding people who made cocaine. No, correction, the work wasn't finding people who made cocaine. The work was finding people who made cocaine who would be willing to speak to us and let us film them.

Our fixer came up trumps. He managed to arrange a meeting with a local coca farmer. This guy was taking a risk talking to us, a prison sentence if he was caught by the cops and something far, far worse, if the local drug cartel found out about it. Basically we were very much in this guy's debt, and however he wanted to conduct the interview, we were going along with it.

That meant beginning our rendezvous on the banks of a very fast-flowing river. Taking our life in our hands, we trusted the local coca farmer, who, armed with a large staff and a knowledge of the river like the back of his hand, was able to lead us across like a contemporary St Christopher, complete with rolled-up trousers. This was a fast, deep, very brown river, and at times we were up to our waists in it, boots around our necks, gritting our teeth, seconds away from being swept away downriver at any given moment. One foot wrong and it was see you later, alligator – or maybe, in this case it was see you later rest of the crew, hello alligator.

Once over, our guide led us across land that we were told did not belong to him, urging us to keep going quickly. Soon, however, we came across the coca leaf. The guy leading us was chewing it all the time, just getting what I can only assume was a mild buzz off it. It's a stimulant, so for low-paid workers like him it was essential to keep going in order to earn his paltry dollar a day. Told to chew, not swallow, I tried a bit. Imagine chewing tea, a bit like that. 'It cheers us up,' said the farmer.

Soon, however, we began to see it within the vegetation of the forest. Carrying on through the mysterious not-my-land, we then came to what I can only describe as a field of coca leaf. The natural growing forest had been burnt away and you could see stumps of trees that had been replaced by coca leaf. Looking at it from that perspective, I stared around at the valleys as we passed through, seeing vast sections of greenery that had been razed and replanted with coca leaf, turning the surrounding countryside into a patchwork.

We came into the farm, the first stage, from which our farmer oversaw the growth of the leaf. Then, we travelled deeper into the jungle, to what they call a piscina.

There we found a family whose job it was to process the coca leaf and produce what is known as cocaine paste. This was the next stage in the production of cocaine.

The first thing I noticed was the smell of chemicals. We were told the coca leaves are left soaking in a trench with water and bleach for ten hours, then trodden, like grapes for wines by the kids wearing Wellington boots. The concentrate from the trampled leaf is mixed with kerosene to separate the drug from the rest of the leaf. They then add ammonia and chalk. Instantly we saw the colour change to white. Next the solution was filtered, leaving just the paste. To me, the whole thing looked like making cheese.

And then we watched as, quite casually, drums full of kerosene and ammonia were emptied and the chemicals simply drained into the river. Litres of acid, kerosene and bleach. It's estimated 15 million litres of toxic fluids, including sulphuric acid, quicklime acetone and kerosene gets flushed into the river systems every year as a direct result of cocaine production. Here it was, happening before our very eyes.

We left, dismayed, but having done what we came there to do, which was get the footage we needed.

After an epic journey slipping and sliding through the mud we eventually got back to our van. By this time our driver was really skittish, worried about paramilitaries, the armies, the drug cartels, and still freaked out about the kid mud-surfing in front of the van. To him we represented the ultimate in bad luck charms and we got the sense that he literally couldn't wait to get rid of us.

We placated him, returned to our hotel and there, in the corner was my lovely pile of wet and muddy clothes to which I added a set of, if you can believe it, *even wetter* and *even muddier* clothes. There was no hot water in the room, none in Tom's room either, although Will the cameraman had a bit. (And if you're wondering why the cameraman often gets the biggest room, that's because he has to carry the heaviest, most unwieldy kit around all day and then, at the end of the day, when the rest of us are popping off to the bar, he's often working into the wee small hours charging kit, downloading footage on to memory cards, transferring memory cards to hard drives, stuff like that. We work on the assumption that we are in constant danger of having our footage nicked, impounded or confiscated and so, without going into too many details – I'm tapping the side of my nose here – we have to take certain precautions to minimise the risk. So, yes, for those reasons the cameraman gets the best room. And on this occasion it meant getting the one room that had some form of hot water.) Clearly I have a major case of room anxiety . . .

That night, as we did every night, we went to the fried chicken place. We sat on plastic chairs at plastic tables with bottles of beer on the table in front of us while rain pelted down on a corrugated iron roof above our heads and an old lady sat in the corner regarding us with one evil eye. Every now and then the electricity would go off. Then come back on again, then go off again. At any given second you might be plunged into darkness.

The weird thing was that I never got sick of eating fried chicken and chips, because during the day we didn't eat anything apart from energy bars, so the fried chicken and chips came as a delicious treat in the evening. That and a beer, Skol, which it usually is in that part of the world. You can drink tons of it and never get drunk.

Meanwhile, in my room, the pile of clothes grew. There were leaks all over the place, water running through the room. So my clothes were getting *even wetter* than they already were. The shower also leaked, so that only made the situation worse when I had my (cold) shower.

Drawing towards the end of our visit we hooked up with local military. Because the demand for cocaine worldwide has grown so much, and because so much of it comes from Peru, the world has said to Peru, 'Could you do something to stop this, please?' In order to give Peru an incentive to do something, the world gives Peru a lot of money. Peru says, 'Thank you very much' and arms its soldiers with the very best weaponry and the best equipment possible. Meeting these guys, they were tooled up beyond belief, almost all of them wearing shades, some of them tying Rambo-style bandanas around their necks. It was clear that they really meant business.

And with good reason. They have two roles: one is to back up the cops on the ground, the other is to take on Shining Path (see F is for the Fine Art of Travelling Through the Peruvian Jungle Part II). The army believe Shining Path have joined forces with the drug traffickers and are now processing coca themselves, while in return the drug traffickers rely on the terrorists for project protection which, they say, has contributed to the growing wave of terrorism in the area.

We joined the soldiers on a training exercise and went up in an army helicopter. From our new vantage point we could see even more clearly the destruction wreaked by the growing of the coca leaf. We saw farmers lying out coca leaves to dry in the sun, the very first stage in the process. The army was taking no action, though. That was for another day.

Could we join them on a raid of a cocaine factory? we asked. Yes, we were told. No problem at all.

So the next day we met up with our army friends once again. Same guys, same Rambo-style bandanas, same dark sunglasses hiding implacable stares. The lot of us bundled on to flatbed trucks and off we went, speeding through the Vrae Valley, with our van keeping up the rear.

Fair enough, the roads in that part of the world all look pretty similar. See one road winding through the Peruvian rainforest and you've seen them all. It's not as if there's a huge amount to differentiate them. But even so, sitting on the back of the flatbed truck, I started to get the feeling that we had come this way before.

On the film you hear me on the narration saying that I am getting suspicious. What happened was that I was sitting on the back of a flatbed truck, in contact with the director, Ewen Thomson, who was with the cameraman Will in the Toyota van, the nervous driver in the driving seat. I was doing little pieces to camera, so they were able to hear what I was saying but I couldn't hear what they were saying. So everything I said, Ewen had to respond in a kind of sign language.

Although this particular sign language, whatever kind of sign language it was, wasn't anything I actually understood. So the way the conversation went was like this:

Me: 'This is fucking weird, I'm sure this is where we came the other day.'

Ewen: [some weird hand gesture I don't understand]

Me: 'Ewen, I'm really not sure about this.'

Ewen: [some weird hand gesture I don't understand]

Me: 'Ask him, ask the driver where he thinks we're going.'

But then I caught sight of the driver. He was full on, eyes as wide as saucers, knuckles white on the steering wheel.

Even from my position sitting on the back of a bumpy flatbed truck way ahead of him, I could tell this guy was terrified.

Shit.

We were going back to the same cocaine factory. The very same cocaine factory we had been taken to the other day. The guy who'd taken us there, the farmer, the people we met at the factory – they'd all put their necks on the line for us. How was it going to look if we returned with a bunch of Rambo-style army motherfuckers?

I tell you how it was going to look. It was going to look bad. It was going to look bad for those guys who'd be in trouble with whoever they answered to – no doubt some fairly nasty guys – for breaching the code of silence, and it was going to look bad for us, because we'd be seen as having blatantly informed on the guys who ran the factory.

The trucks stopped by the side of the road, virtually at the same point where we'd met St Christopher a few days before. We jumped out with the interpreter and spoke to the soldiers. The commander confirmed we were going back to the same place.

Shit. Double shit.

By now our driver was having absolute kittens. If it was going to be bad for us then it would be twice as bad for him. The rate we were going we were going to get him killed and no film is worth somebody's life.

Urgent conversations were held. God bless our fixer. He did a tremendous job somehow managing to juggle me, getting more and more agitated, saying, 'No way, absolutely no way are we going back there' and the soldiers, unreadable behind their Ray-Bans, their faces steely and remorseless. The whole time my mind was chewing over the possibilities: had someone in the chain grassed somebody up? Maybe just a local who'd seen us the day we met the coca-leaf farmer.

Either way, that information had reached the army and now they were taking us back there. Why? Who knows. To send a message, perhaps. A message that you can't expect to collaborate with gringos making documentaries and get away with it. Or to send us a message. That you can't come over here with the cameras expecting to do whatever you want without consequences.

Well, if that was the message then it was received loud and clear as we sweated by the side of the road that morning. I was more than aware of the consequences. I was shitting consequences.

In the end, what we agreed was that we would not raid this particular factory. The one we visited the other day was safe. Instead we'd go to another one.

The cold-eyed army commander spoke to our translator who relayed the information back to us. We could go to this other one, he said, but the other one was near a village and there might be . . . *trouble*.

To be honest, we weren't sure what he meant by that – 'trouble'. Still, we went along with it. And off we drove to a new cocaine factory. We crept through the forest when suddenly dogs began barking. These were the early warning systems for the factory and sure enough, when we arrived we found the place completely deserted, apparently vacated about five minutes previously. Whoever was there, they weren't there now – all that was left were some shacks, coca leaves left out to dry ready for processing, and the usual apparatus for cocaine making.

This, the army guys destroyed. We watched as they tipped out the chemicals, flooding them once again into the water table. Poisoning it. They had no choice, the army guys assured us. But I began to wonder, watching them at work, who exactly was benefiting from this entire operation? Nobody was arrested. The cocaine making would continue. Well, we knew who the victim was. As we watched poisonous water trickle down into what should have been pure-water rivers, as we saw soldiers setting fire to the wooden crates used as part of the process, it was clear that the victim was the environment.

And of course the nearby village. What quickly became apparent was that the village depended on this particular cocaine factory for their livelihoods. What's more, this particular village had a rather important geographical position. It lay between us and, well, the rest of the world.

And the soldiers knew it. Basically, they'd done us up like kippers. To pay us back for messing up the earlier operation, they'd made us the public face of this raid and put us at the mercy of the angry villagers.

We heard shots fired. Stones were thrown. We were most certainly not welcome.

The soldiers dropped us back at our vehicles and that was it – 'adios amigos', you're on your own now. After some almost comical discussion about trying to float the van downriver on a raft, we ended up driving back with our heads down and arrived back at our hotel in San Francisco, temporarily safe and sound, but knowing we were far from out of the woods.

We were in big trouble now: the army hated us because we'd stuffed up their plan of raiding the first cocaine factory; the local people hated us because they thought we were in league with the army. If we stayed there was every chance that we were going to get killed. So we came up with a plan: we decided to do a moonlight flit. We'd already decided we could sort out the driver. He would need to be relocated – just as soon as we made our escape.

So. 4 a.m. Everybody set their mobile phones, watch alarms, whatever. We'd told people in San Francisco that we were staying for another four or five days, we'll see you tomorrow for a beer and fried chicken and chips, thank you very much, lulling them into a full sense of security, and then we went to bed as normal.

At 4 a.m. the alarms went off and we got up. From the other rooms I could hear the other guys making a right racket. I'm the smallest out of the lot of us, which has its advantages in a place like Peru – you don't bang your head on the low ceilings of hotels, for a start. That lot weren't so fortunate, though. Stumbling around in the dark they were hitting their heads, shouting with pain, knocking into things. It was like listening to the Three Stooges trying to be quiet.

Bang.

'*Shush!*'

Bang.

'*Ow!*'

I was just thinking to myself, 'For Christ's sake, guys, try and keep it down, will you? Try and be professional. We're trying to do a moonlight flit here, not re-enact the attack on Pearl Harbor,' when it struck me I had no clean top to wear. I had trousers but no top.

I cast the beam of my head torch at the pile of wet and muddy clothes in the corner, a filthy mound of pants, socks, shirts, cheesy feet, crotch rot and thrush all mixed together nicely. I didn't want to go in there but I knew I had to retrieve a shirt.

I plunged my arms into the depth of the pile.

And then started screaming.

What I hadn't realised was that by leaving these clothes to go mouldy in the corner of my room I had basically built a mini-San Francisco – for cockroaches. And when I dug my arms in to try and reach out a T-shirt I found myself under attack. Huge cockroaches were scuttling up my arms to my shoulders, around my back and across my chest. In seconds I was besieged by the bastards. Revolting things, they dropped down my pants, right into the crack of my arse and in my groin. That was the worst thing. Everything else paled into insignificance by the fact that I suddenly had cockroaches swarming around my private parts, and with another shout, I desperately began trying to rip off my trousers.

Only, I was doing everything too fast, and because I was panicking and because there was wet all over the floor of the hotel room and my boots had mud all over them, I slipped and fell on my arse.

My fall was as loud and ungainly as only the fall of a man being attacked by cockroaches can be, and the rest of the crew hurtled in only to find me literally pulling cockroaches out of my trousers, three-inch long monsters that had left pincer marks on the inside of my leg and God knows where else.

I can't even remember what I grabbed to put on, but I grabbed something and then, *at last*, we all piled into the van and headed for the bridge out of town.

The sun was coming up as we trundled over the bridge and back towards the Andes for a seven-hour drive that would eventually take us back to Lima. And we breathed a collective sigh of relief. Well, everyone else did. Me, I was still finding cockroaches in my bag and in my clothes, and I was chucking them out of the van as we drove. We left a trail of them behind us – all the way to San Francisco.

I is for I Can See What You're Up to, Mate

f I've learnt one thing making the films it's that I look like a right numpty in shorts. Tried them in Brazil and Jamaica, never again: I looked like an ex-rugby-playing scoutmaster on a public outing. It just doesn't cut it with gang members.

Still, as bad outfits go, my shorts weren't quite as bad as Marta's get-up when we were in Jamaica for an episode of *Gangs*.

This was series three, so by now Marta had risen to the position of assistant producer. She still did virtually the same job, just got paid more, but that's OK because she's one of the best fixers in the business, and as usual was doing her job with aplomb. On this particular occasion, she'd arranged for me to interview a Jamaican gangster don known only as Little Man. An elusive guy, of course, but Marta had persuaded him to talk to us, and he'd agreed to meet us at a 'secret' location near his home, which turned out to be a disused house five miles outside Kingston.

We arrived and got set up. Lounging on a plastic seat in the middle of a derelict outhouse was Little Man, who wore a bandana (as always – I've lost count of the number of blokes in bandanas I've interviewed) and a woollen beanie hat. Standing around were his goons, similarly dressed in the beanie hat and bandana ensemble, but unlike Little Man who, though I assumed he was armed, kept his piece out of sight, they had weapons on show. Not just any old weapons either. We're talking assault rifles: AK-47s. Proper firepower.

Little Man had a main bodyguard, the proud owner of a long-barrelled Glock 19, which is a prestigious firearm in that part of the world. The bodyguard wore a skull and crossbones belt buckle, just in case you were in doubt about his ultimate bad assedness. And no, if you're wondering, we were in no doubt about his ultimate bad assedness.

One thing I've noticed doing the *Gangs* series is that it's hardly ever the biggest bloke who's leader of the gang. The leader is the one who makes the gang survive, and that's generally because he's the brightest – so whether he's the biggest or smallest is immaterial. He may have to fight and undoubtedly he needs to be tough, but the most important thing for a gang leader is to make the right decisions.

Never was this more true than with Little Man. Not only was he a 'little man' but he was a classic example of a leader who knew that his position involved, as he put it, 'showing them a lot of love'. He even called himself 'a defender of freedom and justice for the youth'. Although, needless to say, his definition of justice differed slightly from most courts.

He'd agreed to the interview on condition that we did something to disguise his voice. On the film he has a slow, laconic voice but in reality he spoke with a lisp. And that's something else I've noticed about gang leaders: how many of them speak with a lisp. Maybe it's the lisp that makes them tough in the first place. For now though, he was quiet, and sat patiently waiting for the interview to begin, regarding us carefully.

Now, to be fair to Marta, it was even more gasping hot than usual that day. Me, I was still oblivious to the fact that shorts on me were a bad look, so I was wearing a pair, as were the other guys on the crew, while Marta was wearing a summer dress, perfect for watching a centre-court clash at Wimbledon, not so perfect for downtown Kingston.

And though the features of the gang members were obscured by their bandanas and beanie hats I could see where their eyes were going. And they were going to Marta's legs.

To understand what took place you have to picture how we were arranged: me and Little Man perched on plastic chairs in the blazing Jamaican heat; three bodyguards behind Little Man, posing with their guns, and slightly in front of them was my soundman James who held his boom to catch everything Little Man said. Beside him was Marta, while behind my left shoulder Andy the cameraman filmed as we spoke, his camera trained on Little Man.

In other words, I was the only one of our crew able to see what happened next.

The bodyguard with the skull and crossbones belt

buckle had the long-barrelled 9mm, and from the corner of my eye I saw the barrel begin to rise. Only, he wasn't pointing it at anybody. Instead he was using it to very, very slowly and carefully, lift the back of Marta's dress.

Marta, bless her, was completely absorbed in her job and I guess when you're wearing a dress like that, and feeling no noticeable change in temperature down below, you're completely oblivious to what was happening. I could imagine Skull and Crossbones smirking beneath his bandana, though his eyes remained steady. Not far away another gang member, the one wielding an AK-47, looked over and so did his mate. Bear in mind, this is during the actual interview. And these guys just didn't care. Why would they? They've got the guns. What did we have? Nothing. We were a bunch of media luvvies from London.

Meanwhile Skull and Crossbones' barrel was rising. And that's not a double entendre, by the way. The barrel of his Glock was rising, and the back of Marta's skirt was going with it.

His eyes were now on me. Taunting me? Daring me? You could see it in their eyes what they were thinking: *let's see how far we can go with this.*

Gradually I realised that the responsibility lay with me and that I only had one card to play.

I leaned forward and said to Little Man, 'You got a mum – you got a mother, yeah?'

He reared back slightly, taken aback by the unexpected question, then nodded slowly, his eyes watchful.

Hoping I looked a lot braver than I felt, I fixed him with

my best stare. 'Well, did your mother bring you up to be that disrespectful?'

And he knew. Even though Little Man couldn't see exactly what was going on, he knew.

Which is another thing I have to say is characteristic of gang leaders – nothing happens without their knowledge. He knew *exactly* what was going on. There was a brief pause. One of those pauses where you think, this could go either way. Then he looked over to Skull and Crossbones, clicked his fingers and like that the gun barrel was withdrawn and Marta's skirt fell back into place.

The interview continued, and was very good in the end, with Marta puzzling over what had been said, but otherwise none the wiser about what had gone on.

I told her when we got back to our hotel. Phased? Not our Marta.

J is for John Mongrel, 'Interesting Guy'

'A soft face' – it was a term I first came across in Cape Town's Pollsmoor Prison, making what turned out to be a BAFTA-winning episode of *Gangs*.

I was in Pollsmoor to investigate South Africa's infamous Numbers gang. Weirdly sexualised, riddled with all kinds of ritualistic customs and very, very powerful indeed, the Numbers are one of the most downright strange and scary gangs I've ever encountered.

What makes them unique is the fact that they're a purely prison-based gang. Since the 1980s their tendrils of power have extended outside of Pollsmoor and they've forged strong links with gangs in Cape Town's fierce Cape Flats region (see also W is for a trip to the White House), but Pollsmoor remains their centre of operations.

Under the guidance of senior warder Chris Malgas, I was to learn a great deal more about the Numbers during my tours of Pollsmoor. I would also come into contact with one of the most genuinely frightening and fearsome men I've ever met, a bloke who in many ways I have to thank, for meeting him helped me earn my journalistic spurs.

The weird thing about Pollsmoor is that it's in a fairly well-to-do area of countryside not far outside Cape Town. You approach the prison via roads that pass vineyards, beautiful market gardens and smart housing. Based on everything I'd heard about Pollsmoor – that it was a hell on earth, a place where the warders were hugely outnumbered and barely in charge, a place where rape and violence were a daily occurrence – my mind had conjured post-apocalyptic scenes ripped straight out of *The Road*. But driving through this scenic countryside and, what's more, knowing that there was a golf course next door – well, I couldn't help but wonder if its reputation hadn't been exaggerated.

Despite the beautiful view on the way to the prison, from the moment I saw the grey blocks of Pollsmoor squatting on the horizon I could tell it was a dark, heartless place, and my instincts were proved correct.

As I entered the inside of the prison with Chris Malgas at my side he explained to me the divisions within the Numbers gang: the 28s are the fighters, the 27s are the assassins, the 26s are the moneymen – but they all kill and rape.

We came to what they call the admissions yard. Most of the prisoners in Pollsmoor are awaiting trial. That means two things: firstly, there are a massive amount of prisoners coming in and out each day, around 300 men. Secondly, there is far less emphasis on rehabilitation and thus fewer resources, prison programmes and so forth. It's one of the reasons gang culture is so rife there: there's literally nothing else to do. Even exercise is outlawed, because that's when the gang members can talk to one another.

In the admissions yard we watched as new arrivals were forced to line up naked, then come forward, squat, as if they were about to take a shit, then bounce up and down on their haunches a couple of times.

What was all that about?

The watching guards were 'looking for the poke', Chris told me.

'The poke?'

The poke, it turned out, is a plastic tube that convicts stick up their arse to hold money, drugs, weapons, whatever. And the idea of the squat is to dislodge a poke and stop them taking it into the prison. It's a degrading and humiliating process. What's worse, those who try smuggling a poke into Pollsmoor are not even doing it for themselves, they're being forced to take it in by other, higher-ranking prisoners. Numbers, in other words.

This, for many, is where the trouble starts. Refuse to take the poke and you'll be punished. Standard punishment for refusing to take the poke? They cut out an eye. After that I'm guessing you don't refuse a second time.

And if, as is inevitable, you do take the poke, well, then your troubles have *really* begun. Evade the taking-a-shit procedure in the admissions centre and you'll be told to take yourself off to one of the Numbers, who retrieve the poke. Sometimes the poke gets stuck. Won't come out easily. When that happens – and look away now if you're of a squeamish disposition – they fish it out using a coat hanger.

Thus, possibly, begins your new career as a prison 'wyfie'.

'A wyfie has to give the Number man who owns him sex when he wants it,' explained Chris. 'He has to wash the Number's clothes, cook his food, clean for him and do everything his Number master tells him to do.'

'And what if he tries to resist?'

'They will either beat him or kill him. A 27 assassin comes to kill him on the orders of the 28s.'

In other words the new arrivals were almost certainly staring down a future of sex slavery, serial rape, beatings and murder. Little wonder they all looked so terrified.

Tattoos are everywhere. Called chappies, they're carved with razor blades then filled in with biro ink. It's one of the ways in which gang members are able to identify each other. One prisoner I spoke to had a rather charming tattoo of two men having sex across his back.

Every now and then I would hear a piercing shriek or a blood-curdling shout. I often say that the worst screams I've ever heard are those of a bereaved mother – it's another story, and I heard way too many of those while in Juarez in Mexico – but the disembodied howls I heard in Pollsmoor came a close second. I found my eyes travelling up, up to the identical, barred windows overlooking the admissions yard wondering what atrocities were occurring within the bowels of the prison. The ratio of guards to prisoners is apparently around 1 to 100, and the guards can't even carry guns in case of them being snatched by convicts. I quickly reached the conclusion that any control the warders had was tenuous at best. The prison officers walked a razor line every day and night. Inside the Numbers were in charge.

As for them – I've never encountered such a ritualised organisation in my life. I couldn't even begin to describe the strange rules and initiations that govern them. There were some 27s who could only ever stand in the shade and never moved in daylight. Wyfies have to sit silent and face the cell wall when members of the Number are present. They have to do what the Number owner wants straightaway, clean their cell, cut their toenails, God knows what else, and the only way to escape that living hell was through violence: stab a guard or kill another gang member, literally *fight* to gain the respect required to rise up the ranks.

Moving on through the prison we went to the security wing where some of the more dangerous gang members were kept. Chris stopped me. For the first time I saw a little nervousness in his eyes, just a little, as he told me, 'Remember: you focus, you keep a soft face, you breathe, you make eye contact and you think. You never show fear. The Numbers are pack animals: if you show them fear, they are on top of you.'

Yes, there it was, the 'soft face' – and it was then that it struck me that during my entire time in the prison I hardly ever saw an actual human emotion. The soft face – it could have meant a hard face or a stony face. It was an expression to mean a complete lack of expression.

Mirrors were poked through the bars of cells as we made our way along the wing. There I met more members of the Numbers gang, always intensely aware that we were out on a limb here. What if they overpowered Chris and took us hostage?

Keep a soft face, Ross, I kept telling myself. Keep a soft face. I was shown makeshift weapons: huge padlocks fastened to knife-sharp belts or straps, a tin mug with a sharpened rim tied to a belt, but of course if they really wanted to do serious damage then the victim would be stabbed to death.

It was during our fourth visit to Pollsmoor that we got to meet the infamous John Mongrel.

I often get people asking me what's the worst place I've ever visited. What was hell? And the answer is: it's all relative. If you're claustrophobic then hell is being locked in a cupboard. I daresay there are those who thrived within the walls of Pollsmoor. Likewise, of the many gangsters, terrorists and militia men I've had the pleasure of interviewing, who was the baddest? Who was the most evil?

Again, who can say? I can barely think of anybody I've met who hasn't felt justified in doing what they do. For whatever reason, whether they think they are avenging wrongs done to themselves, their families, their people; whether they think they're protecting their homeland, standing up for their rights – I'd wager there are very few of them who look in the mirror and see the bad guy.

John Mongrel, though. Him I'm not sure about.

This was 2006 and he'd already been in Pollsmoor for nineteen years. The first nine were for a murder he committed aged fourteen. The next ten for the murder of an inmate inside. Rumour has it he's out now and possibly even a reformed character, for which I'm supremely thankful, because the John Mongrel I met was about as far from a reformed character as it's possible to get. There was something about him. Something strange and terrifying and, yes, maybe even evil. The look of him for a start, as though he had been carved out of wood, his eyes, like those of a shark, and the calm, measured way he spoke, with none of the braggadocio of a gangster, nor any regret – just a sort of *nothing* as he told me what he did.

We got to talk to him because we were looking for somebody to represent the 28s, somebody who would speak about them on camera. Most guys in the prison were terrified of speaking out, and with good reason, the penalty for doing so being death. But John Mongrel had, in his two decades inside, risen up the ranks of the Numbers. One look at him and it was easy to see why. As a general, I guess he had special privileges. He was allowed to speak.

My two guards left the room, leaving me alone with him. When he lent forward I caught a whiff of his breath: a rancid mix of roadkill, nicotine and sour body fluids. He hadn't seen a dentist in a long time, if ever, and you could cut his breath with a knife.

I asked him how he had become involved with the Numbers and calmly, with the piercing stare that was his trademark, he told me that he had strangled and stabbed a man. He went on to say that he gave the orders in Pollsmoor – if there was a warden who was 'not right' then John Mongrel decided whether he lived or died. Gang members who refused to follow his orders were killed. New inmates would be brought to his cell.

'And if he is not the Number, I have sex with him.'

I did my best to maintain my 'soft face'.

'How do you have sex with him? You hold him down?'

'I hold him down. My face to face.'

Did having sex with men mean he was gay? I asked him.

His look left me in no doubt what he thought of that particular suggestion. No, he told me, he was not gay. He was a man. The wyfie was gay.

Mongrel told me how he sharpened a toothbrush into a lethal weapon by heating it up then honing it to a fine point on the stone floor. He described killing a man, having other 28s hold the victim down while he first shoved the point of the sharpened toothbrush in between his ribs then used his feet to stamp it into the heart as hard as he could.

He described what happened after he killed his first warden. He was put in solitary confinement where the wardens came for him in the night. They beat him so badly he was knocked unconscious. Despite what you might see in films this is no mean feat. In real life, you have to beat somebody very, very badly in order for them to lose consciousness. Mongrel made me touch his skull, which felt soft and springy beneath my fingers, a memento of the beating. After leaving him almost for dead the guards put him on a diet of millet and water for six weeks. The thing about millet is that the human body cannot digest it at first. You have to chew it, pass it out in your shit, wash it with water (if you have any water) then eat it all over again. Only by eating it the second time around does the millet give you enough nourishment to keep you alive.

It's a circle of brutality with no end and no beginning. As an outsider all you can do is pray you never find your way on to the treadmill.

The whole time we were talking – and we spoke for several hours – he was so scarily matter of fact about the atrocities he had done and continued to do, the abuse that had been heaped upon him, that I began to wonder whether the man opposite me was simply an out-and-out psychopath. Perhaps he had been completely dehumanised by what he had done and what had been done to him.

However, talking to him was a great learning experience. I quickly realised that an interview is as much about getting the subject to relax, to open up, as it is about asking questions. And you do that by chatting to them in a non-judgemental way. Nowadays when I do an interview I have a rough idea of what I want to ask, what I want from the interview and what we're seeking to explain to the audience. But aside from that I go with the flow. I talk to the subject. And I make sure I don't judge.

John Mongrel also taught me the value of patience. When I interviewed him, I didn't jump straight in with the big questions. I learnt the value of sitting back, in this case for some four hours, and establishing a rapport.

So, yes, in a way he taught me something. As I said to camera coming out of the interview, 'John Mongrel, interesting guy.' What else could you say?

K is for Kit and Caboodle

We carry up to twenty-five bags of kit on any given film: lenses, mini-cranes, tripods, camera bodies, and boxes and boxes of camera equipment. So as far as personal luggage goes, we try and keep it to a minimum. Here's a few of the essentials that get packed in my rucksack every time.

Boots

And flip-flops, all right? (See B is for Be Careful Where You . . .), and a plentiful supply of socks too. Flip-flops for my down time to get air to my poor old plates of meat. One thing you have to look after is your feet.

Cigarette lighters

Because it's handy to have but also because if you're interviewing someone and they stick a cigar, a cigarette or a spliff in their mouth, you can offer them a light. It's amazing how much goodwill you can get that way.

Energy bars

Lots of days, this is all we eat. It's one of the reasons we were so glad just for the chicken and chips in San Francisco (the one in Peru).

A hat
Or a head scarf, or a bandana of some kind, something to protect your head in hot climates, bald heads in particular.

Hostile-Environment Training
You have that before you go out. It's common sense to get it, although you have to have it for insurance purposes, and you have to update it regularly, too.

A good knife
Obviously be careful where you carry it and where you take it. You don't want to be walking around the streets of a city carrying a knife, but if you're in the jungle, have two knives in case you lose one.

Medical kit
And it's a good idea to make sure you know how to use the contents as well.

Mosquito repellent/nets
When it comes to mosquito spray, Deet is the stuff. It'll melt your watchstrap, but it works.

Suntan lotion
Particularly for my head. The higher the factor the better; I'm not there on holiday.

Sweets
To raise morale and occasionally make friends.

Torch/head torch

Both are essential, and plenty of batteries, of course.

Water

And chlorine tablets to purify the water or a flask with a charcoal filter. The chlorine tablets make the water taste disgusting – like drinking a swimming pool, basically – but at least you reduce your chances of getting D&V (see S is for (I love the) Smell of Shit Pits in the Morning).

Wet wipes

Preferably antiseptic, for the occasional shit in the woods.

L is for Lost in Translation

Visiting the Democratic Republic of the Congo for *Extreme World* wasn't exactly a laugh-a-minute experience. And what laughs we did have were after the event, rather then during it, our hellish stay in Walikale being a prime example (see A is for *Avez-Vous Le Boeuf?*).

Another example was meeting the Mayi-Mayi, a militia set up to defend themselves against other militia. These are the guys who, when I spoke to them, told me they drank a herbal potion that made them bulletproof, and while I'm not one to judge – and certainly not when it comes to cultures I know so little about – I think I can safely say they were misguided on that score.

Tempting, then, to think of them as a bit backward? A bit simple? Not a bit of it. It doesn't matter where you go in the world, people love a piss-take and, as it turned out, the Mayi-Mayi were no different. Arriving at a parade ground near to the community we were treated to what we thought was a charming traditional African welcome of singing and chanting.

Having got our footage we thought the translation was

this: 'The white man is filming us but we are watching him, we are watching him. The white man is filming us but we are watching him, we are filming him.'

However, when we had the film double-checked prior to transmission – and bloody lucky that we did – what emerged was a slightly different version. A remix, if you like. The cheeky boys and girls had changed the lyric halfway through. Anybody watching who understood the dialect they were using would have heard this: 'The white man fucked us all night, never paid us a thing.'

Oops.

Some judicious editing of the piece was required in order to remove the offending lyrics, and we breathed a huge sigh of relief, while secretly congratulating the Mayi-Mayi on a cracking practical joke.

M is for Minefield (or Mind Out the Way, Mark McCauley)

Despite the rather flippant title, I still – after all these years – feel like a right nob for what I did to our cameraman, Mark. In my defence, I was operating on a kind of 'fight or flight' mechanism – specifically the 'flight' bit of it.

It all happened during the making of the second series of *Afghanistan*, when I was with 45 Commando, Victor Company, Fire Support Group in Kajaki and moving up on a hill adjacent to a Taliban stronghold known as the Big Top. The FSG's job is to provide covering fire for troops on the ground, and doing that means making good use of elevated positions. But of course the Taliban know that, so the hills are seeded with IEDs. One marine had already tragically lost his life to one.

Once an area is designated free of IEDs it's marked with white powder, and as we moved up the hill we were warned that the only safe path was between the white lines. Whatever we did, we had to stay between the lines.

Going was slow as we trudged up the hill. At the bottom was the Jackal, an armoured vehicle. In front of me was Sven and Scotty of the FSG, behind me was Mark, filming.

And then it happened. We were stopped by the command, 'Back off'. The marines had discovered a large IED with a command wire attached. We began to retreat to the foot of the hill. At the same time the enemy opened fire. I heard the zip of automatic gunfire, the unmistakeable feel of rounds parting the air close to the top of my head and, knowing we were hideously exposed, I turned and ran.

I barrelled straight into Mark, knocked him over before going sprawling myself. From behind I heard shouts, the bang of gunfire and the whistle of rounds passing overhead and I picked myself up and kept on running. The kind of running I was doing, they call it the swastika, because of the shape of your arms and legs. And I swastika'd right down that hill, just as fast as I could.

Two things I should have done.

Number one, I should have stayed between the white lines.

'Ross! Stay on the track!' roared Sven from behind me, but it wasn't until I saw the footage later that I even heard him. At the time I was concentrating on reaching the Jackal. And no way was I remembering to stay between the white lines. I zig-zagged my way down the slope until I made it to the safety of the Jackal, and nothing but dumb luck stopped me stepping right on to an IED.

Number two: I should have stopped to pick Mark up, especially as it was me who'd knocked him over in the first place. As it was, Sven hauled him up and picked up the camera so filming could continue and Mark made it to the Jackal safely. But yeah – I didn't stop to help my mucker up. What can I say other than self-preservation got the better of me, and, well . . . sorry, Mark.

N is for Never Walk Around the Back of a Helicopter

M any moons ago, in 1999, when a younger, more innocent Ross was preparing to leave the cloistered environs of *EastEnders* at Elstree and set sail for ITV, I took part in a documentary called *Ross Kemp Alive in Alaska*.

As far as the TV side of things was concerned, I suppose you'd have to say that *Alive in Alaska* was a precursor to *I'm a Celebrity Get Me Out of Here*, where they'd stick a well-known face in the back of beyond and watch them try to survive. Lenny Henry did one. Joanna Lumley did another. And Billy Connolly did *A Scot in the Arctic*.

And from a 'me' point of view – well, like I say, it marked the point at which I began to establish a separate identity away from Grant and *EastEnders*, and it gave me a taste for documentary making and adventure.

It also taught me something useful about helicopters.

My *Alive in Alaska* experience began in a helicopter, the plan being to land in the Klondike somewhere. I wasn't on my own – not at that stage of the game anyway – there was a cameraman and a soundman who had been taken up on a previous run, the idea being that they would film me as I was dropped off. Nor was I going in completely green; I'd had some cold-weather training to prepare me.

Still, my heart sank as I stared out of the helicopter windows, seeing snow and ice and spindly trees as far as the eye could see and knowing that whatever training I'd had, it could never prepare me for the reality. It would be true of Afghanistan, true for *Extreme World* – for which we have to have regular hostile-environment training – and it was true of Alaska. Bear in mind I was used to pulling pints at the Vic. Suddenly I was being schooled in how to survive the freezing climate – or at least how best to *try* and survive the freezing climate – and thanks to the fact that they'd given me a .375 Winchester (a bear gun!), I was given some weapons training as well.

But nothing about how to deal with helicopters.

And if there had been helicopter training, lesson one would have been: never walk around the back of one when its rotors are turning. Why? Because you don't see the tail rotor turning, it's going so fast. The tail boom just seems to end. You ever wondered why tail rotors are often painted in garish, alternating colours? It's to make them as visible as possible and reduce the hazard for ground crews.

But you can paint the rotor all the colours of the rainbow – paint it in reflective pink neon if you want – and you still won't see it in a whiteout, a blizzard, which was the weather that day. And if you're landing in a blizzard, where you can't hear or see anything and where your senses are completely obliterated by the stinging weather, then it's even more important you don't wander around the back of the helicopter.

So what does muggins here do?

Jumping out of the helicopter, trying to remember that we're filming while also endeavouring to get my backpack, I scrambled out of the helicopter and darted right around the back of it . . .

I didn't see it, obviously. Thanks to the blizzard, I didn't hear it either. But I felt it. A whooshing sound by my ear that stopped me dead in my tracks, and I knew that I'd come *that close* to becoming human coleslaw.

So, bloody dangerous things, tail rotors. If only helicopters could do without them, right?

Fast-forward to 2010, when I made the *Battle for the Amazon* films, and we were flying over the Ecuadorian rainforest so I could do a piece to camera introducing the film and giving the viewer an extraordinary panoramic view of the jungle beneath. Aussie cameraman Steve Lidgerwood, a renowned cameraman and a great guy, was working with me, as well as the soundman, Tim Watts. The director Southan Morris was in the helicopter, too, along with the translator, and – very important, this – the pilot.

Getting the shot we wanted involved me hanging out of the helicopter. Not James Bond-style, but getting strapped into a harness then leaning out of the open door, with my feet on the landing skid. That way the shot was composed of me and the rainforest, rather than a titchy bit of me, a titchy bit of the rainforest and huge chunk of helicopter interior. Because of the size of the helicopter we had to take out the rear window in order to get the shot we needed. It's not unknown – they're designed to come out, after all – but I can tell you this: it doesn't exactly make for a comfortable ride.

Still, sod that. The shot was going to look great. I mean, we were convinced the shot was going to look great and as a result lavished a lot of time on getting it to look good, screaming at each other as we were buffeted by winds and persuading the pilot to hover whenever we could.

Was the hovering to blame for what later happened? I don't know, but I subsequently discovered that despite being built to hover – indeed, being famous for their hovering abilities – helicopters don't actually like to do it. It kind of knackers them out. Especially older helicopters, like this one was.

I'd say we filmed from around 6 a.m. until 11 a.m. The idea was that we'd then fly on to Yasumi to rendezvous with the producer Tom Watson, who'd gone on ahead because there was too much kit to fit in one helicopter. So when the filming eventually finished, that's where we headed.

Perhaps we'd asked too much of the chopper, what with all the hovering and swooping we'd been doing, but as we skimmed across the top of the forest, the nose of the aircraft was just – I don't know how you'd describe it – but I suppose you'd have to say it was 'flicking' a bit. Just every now and then, a little bump that made you start a little but nothing to be concerned about. Or so I thought.

Like I say there were six of us in this bird, but thanks to the current configuration of headphones, only Southan and I could speak to each other without bawling our throats out. He was the director and he'd been directing me for the piece to camera, so it made sense we could speak. Anyway. The nose was doing this flicking thing and suddenly Southan, who by that point was sitting next to the pilot, said, 'Oi, Ross?'

'Yes, mate,' I said.

He was turned in his seat and I got that weird sense of dislocation you get when you can see someone's lips move but the sound comes through your headphones.

'Can you just check the tail rotor is working, mate?' he said.

'Oh, shut up, Southan.'

He's a bit of a wind-up merchant. Was then and probably still is now. And to be honest, I was just not in the mood. We'd been buffeted by the wind all morning, we were all hungry, we were travelling deeper into the Ecuadorian rainforest – it wasn't the time for fun and games.

'No, really,' he said, 'the pilot says can you check if the tail rotor is still working.'

I pulled a face at him. 'You are kidding me?'

As if to make the point the nose of the chopper did its little flick thing.

'Er, no, mate,' said Southan, very seriously, and I could tell by his face he wasn't kidding. The way his face was sort of . . . grey. 'No, mate, I ain't kidding.'

I swallowed something hard and then, still strapped into my waist-harness and with one foot braced on the landing skid, leant out and craned my head to look at the tail rotor.

What I wanted to see was a nice, spinning, coleslaw-making tail rotor. Just like in Alaska.

What I actually saw was a wheezing, sputtering tail rotor. A tail rotor that looked like it was on its last legs.

And the thing is, you *need* a tail rotor. It's not like it's decorative, or a spare little rotor that's handy to have in case the big one gives out. No, what it does is counteract the torque of the main rotor. Which is why, when it started to wheeze and sputter like ours was doing, the nose of the chopper was doing its flicking thing.

And as though to celebrate being noticed at last, the helicopter began to behave even more erratically.

'Yeah?' prompted Southan, who hardly needed an answer, given what the helicopter was now doing.

'It looks fucked,' I told him, using the technical jargon.

Southan went a lighter shade of grey. 'All right,' he said, and conferred with the pilot. 'Pilot says we've got to head back to Coca airport,' he confirmed.

Coca airport was our base.

Looking around the cabin I saw faces that mirrored my own fear. The thing about a broken tail rotor is that the pilot can usually force a crash-landing. It's bad but it doesn't have to be fatal.

If you can land in the right place, that is. And the rainforest is just about the opposite location to the right place. Even if you avoided being impaled by trees on the way down. Even if the helicopter didn't ignite. Even if you weren't mutilated by alligators, poisoned by snakes or bitten by spiders, then how the hell were you going to get out of there when nobody knew where you were?

But as long as the tail rotor kept spinning we'd be OK.

I watched as the pilot, with sweat streaming freely down the side of his face, began desperately twiddling knobs, flicking switches and pressing buttons, doing whatever it was he needed to do to keep the bloody thing in the air. Every now and then I twisted in my seat to look out at the rotor, daring to hope it would suddenly spark back into life properly. My heart sinking when instead of getting better it just seemed to be getting worse.

Next the pilot was calling Mayday – and I really started to panic.

Below us I saw a gas terminal and wondered if the short apron could be used as a makeshift landing pad.

'No,' said the driver, speaking through Southan, 'Can't land there – they won't let you land there if you're a Mayday, because of the risk of explosion.'

'Oh, perfect.'

Fifteen minutes to go. There was plenty of leakage in the cabin as we sweated every second, knowing the tail rotor could conk out any moment now and the chopper begin to descend in what would hopefully be a controlled spin, crashing through the canopy of the wild and untamed rainforest, depositing us into a slow, drawn-out death.

Ten minutes to go, and by now it felt as if the rotor was more off than it was on. I'd look out, see it spinning and wonder if it was actually motorised, or just rotating in the wind, having all the effect of a child's windmill. The pilot contacted Coca to let them know we were about to attempt an emergency landing with a damaged tail rotor, and I imagined the ground crews scrambling into action.

Five minutes to go and through Southan the pilot warned us that he'd be shutting off the engine to land. He didn't actually use the phrase 'controlled crash' but for some reason that's what came to mind.

And then we were coming in to land. We were going to land like a plane, and for a moment it was though we were 'gliding' and very much in the lap of the gods.

And fair play to the pilot, he got us down. It wasn't going to win any awards for comfort and it was very bumpy, but he got us down sliding in on its rails and we scrambled out of the cabin on weak and rubbery legs, to be greeted by the sight of emergency vehicles tearing across the apron towards us. Old-style, 1950s-looking emergency vehicles, they were. Fire engines with clanging bells and guys hanging off the sides, who greeted us as though we'd just returned from a moon landing.

It felt like we had. Still, we now had another problem. Tom was stuck with a tribe that were still killing strangers up until around when I was born. We had no way of telling him to get his arse back. He had no idea we weren't coming. We were stuck in Coca without a brass farthing.

And that, as they say, is another story.

To be continued in . . . T is for a Totemic Tropical Take-Off.

O is for Oh, Is This a Stick-Up?

Thanks to *Afghanistan* I've been shot at a few times, and thanks to *Gangs* I've spoken to countless guys holding guns. But having someone actually point a gun at you with his finger on the trigger is something that I don't want to get used to.

We went to Papua New Guinea (PNG) in 2013, hoping to learn more about this country where violence is so endemic, tribal conflict is a part of everyday life, and drugs and alcohol are such a destructive part of the culture – and where the second biggest business in the whole country is security.

First port of call? A hospital in the capital, Port Moresby, where we found an interesting system in place. Because nearly half the admissions are trauma cases, eating up 40 per cent of the hospital's budget, doctors have instigated a system of 'trauma fines', where anyone admitted as a result of fights or alcohol-related incidents must pay a fee in order to be seen.

The root of the epidemic is a tribal system of 'payback', that same cycle of violence I've seen all over the world.

Everywhere you go people are working out their grudges using guns and knives. For the doctors at the Port Moresby hospital, it was especially frustrating, because for each casualty admitted, they knew they'd have to expect at least one more – the payback for the first one. Then another, and another, and so on.

The further you travel out of Port Moresby, the more feral PNG gets, so understandably we were fairly nervous about leaving the relative safety of the capital and setting off for the Highlands. We knew that attacks from armed bandits called rascals are common. Their modus operandi is to stop cars then rob and rape the occupants. Luckily, we'd made contact with a guy called Mike, a guy who'd once been one of the most wanted rascals in the whole of Papua New Guinea. He had dreads piled high on his head, an old shotgun wound to his face and a long beard, and though he seemed nice enough I had to keep reminding myself that he was probably responsible for some fairly reprehensible deeds; you don't become the most wanted man in PNG for nothing. Oh, and he was also the current major of Madang. Still, it's never too late to change, and by all accounts that was what Mike had done. I thanked God he was the one in the driving seat as we negotiated the increasingly chaotic Mendi highway in order to link up with a convoy five hours drive away.

The bus station we reached – well, I said on the film it was like something out of *Apocalypse Now*, like the last sign-post for civilisation before you step off into the unknown. Around us were bright shining halogen lights strung from rundown shacks, figures moving in the shadows, a sense of desperation in the air. Joining the convoy Mike told me that if anybody ran in front of the car with a gun, the best thing to do was to simply hit him with the vehicle. That was reassuring.

It was about an hour outside the bus station, and we were driving through thick mud in the pitch black, when Mike told me, 'Lock your doors.' Funnily enough, they were already locked. But as our headlights illuminated an overturned oil tanker and ghostly figures loitering by the side of the road, some of them smoking, I saw why he'd given the instruction. Locals, some of them armed with machetes, were looting the oil tanker. They wouldn't rest until it was empty, Mike said as we edged past, several sets of curious eyes on us.

Reaching Goroka in the Eastern Highlands of Papua New Guinea I saw for myself the problems created by home-brewed alcohol. Guys sat around a rudimentary distillery getting absolutely smashed. I mean, I like a drink, but bloody hell, these blokes were totally hammered, and hammered like I'd never seen before. The distillery looked like it could explode at any second, but of course the booze hounds were so trashed they didn't care. You had guys carrying bush knives just completely zonked out – until, that is, something upset them, which was when the violence started. As I watched, three of them started throwing punches, quickly joined by a fourth. It was like the kind of fight you see outside a pub on a Saturday night in Croydon, steaming drunk people throwing wild punches. Except this got worse, and as we made our excuses and left, one of the drinkers came crashing out of the forest, his arm spouting blood from a machete wound. He then tackled a banana tree; felling it and himself in one fell swoop.

The whole feeling I was getting was one of complete lawlessness. Who was in control, I wondered? The answer, apparently, was tribal enforcers, and our fixer, Lucas, reckoned he could set up a meeting with one of the region's most feared tribal enforcers, a rascal called the General.

The General was part of Lucas's tribe, the Siku, and according to Lucas was unpredictable and cunning. Feared by virtually everyone, it was said that during tribal warfare he'd rubbed pigs' blood on his gun prior to a kill.

Even with that kind of billing the General still turned out to be more 'out there' than I could possibly have imagined.

I suppose I should have been more suspicious when, on our way up the hill to meet the General, Lucas started hanging back and told us to go the rest of the way by ourselves. The three of us looked at each other: me, Ed Venner the director/soundman and Jonathan Young the cameraman. But we kept going, joining a path that cut through some shacks before coming up short in a clearing, as a number of men materialised from the jungle in front of us.

There were four of them. At the head was a guy who wore a baseball cap and a camouflage jacket. What's more – and this was *slightly* odd – his face was blacked up, completely covered with black camouflage stick. Why? I don't know. After all, the guy was black in the first place. Maybe it was to stop the glare of the sun, or maybe it was an attempt to disguise his features. Maybe it was because he wanted to appear spooky and weird – in which case, well done, General, you looked spooky and weird.

'Who directed you?' he asked us, looking from me to the crew.

'Lucas,' I replied feebly. 'We were told that we were going to meet some guys who'd been involved in some trouble.'

'That depends on what you want to know,' I was told.

They'd come trailing clouds of weed smoke. They were chewing betel nut, a mild stimulant. I was offered a drag on something I was told was tobacco; I had little choice in the matter, so I had a quick puff, handed it back, then was asked to try betel nut. They were testing me, it seemed.

And then it happened – the General ducked and from behind us appeared four men pointing guns at us: two with bolt-action rifles, the other two with shotguns. They were all blacked up like the General, wearing camouflage, and they ordered us to sit down.

I stared at them. I'm not honestly sure exactly what I was thinking at that point but I did have a strong instinct that I was not going to do as I was told. No way was I going to get down. What was going through my mind was that these guys had raped and killed outsiders in the recent past, men and women.

That was what was going through my mind. So whatever happened, I wasn't going down. I'd rather die quickly with a bullet in me than the alternative.

Around me, one of the General's men had already got

down. Ed stood frozen, as petrified as I was. Jonathan, God love him, kept filming.

Another thing that occurred to me: I'd heard one of the guys with the bolt-action load the rifle. In films, gunmen do the *chk-chk* thing because it looks and sounds good on screen, but in real life, if you're going into a situation like that, you chamber a round *before* you go into action. On the other hand, he could just have been putting one up the spout to freak me out.

'Show us your round,' I told him, grabbing hold of the barrel and pushing it away from me.

By now two of them had turned their attention to me, and one of the guys with the shotgun was being aggressive. He'd come round to the front, jabbing the barrel of the shotgun right in my face and yelling, 'Get down!'

That feeling of not wanting to do as I was told persisted, but it was joined by another feeling. The one of being royally pissed off that this guy was poking a gun in my face.

'You going to kill me?' I asked him. It wasn't the coolest thing to say, but hey.

I grabbed the barrel of the shotgun. I had the bottle of water in one hand, the other holding the barrel, and I advanced on the gunman, making him retreat as I kept repeating, 'Are you going to kill me?'

'Sit down,' he commanded.

'No,' I told him, repeating, 'Are you going to kill me?'

Our eyes locked and he got the message. He realised that there was no way I was going down. It was time to either back off or pull the trigger.

He stood down. And almost as quickly as it had kicked off, the situation seemed to defuse: on the General's command the four guys lowered their weapons. The guy with the shotgun even smiled.

I was babbling, 'No one's going to fucking kill me,' which, again, might not have been the coolest thing in the world to say, but I was riding a major hit of adrenalin and was in no fit state to be cool, so you'll have to forgive me.

'You're very courageous,' said the General, after I had assured him I wasn't going down, not for anyone.

Looking back now, what I see is myself in a state of shock, at first pretending the whole thing wasn't really happening – quite casually taking a swig of water – then realising that I had to do something or risk putting myself, Ed and Jonathan at their mercy, which I was sure was the worst thing possible to do.

Was it a set up just to intimidate us? I don't know. Maybe they wanted to rile us up. Maybe they wanted to show us how strong and powerful they were. Or maybe they planned to steal the camera and kill us. I'm not sure. If it was prearranged then it was clear not all of the General's men were in on the joke, because at least one of them had hit the deck when the gunmen arrived.

Whatever their motives, I still feel angry about what happened, but all I know is that afterwards we got a great interview from the General, who was clearly an intelligent man. But I guess if I've learnt anything from these films it's to expect the unexpected and to definitely come up with a better line than 'Oh, is this a stick-up?'

P is for a Prostitute Called Margarita

Among the delights of Venezuela are lovely chocolate and beautiful women. But like everywhere in the world it's a country with a huge wealth gap. Take a seat in one of the more expensive hotels in its capital, Caracas, and you could be in Miami or Los Angeles: the atmosphere, the service, the food – it's all good.

Go a short distance, though (and not even *that* short a distance, see Z is for Zebra Crossings in Venezuela) and you'll witness desperate poverty and crime first-hand. Where you get poverty you get drugs and crime, and in the barrios of Caracas, drugs and crime are alive and kicking, believe you me.

We were there for an episode of *Extreme World* and, as is often the case, began by visiting a local hospital, in this case the Pérez de León. Within five minutes of turning up on a Friday evening, two bodies were being carted in. They were an off-duty policeman and his wife who had had been sitting in a car, both shot dead. Not a pretty sight.

Next a girl arrived who'd been shot in the leg. I stood and watched with a mixture of horror, admiration and bemusement as medical staff got to work, cleaning up the wound and delivering little lectures about the dangers of hanging around barrios with the wrong sorts. I'd hazard a guess that they were more than usually stingy with the pain relief for cases they considered less worthy. In fact, I think the message was, 'If you're going to hang around drinking in barrios, then you risk getting involved in a drive-by and shot. And now I'm going to stick my thumb in the wound, just to make sure the bullet hole has been cleaned with iodine and, of course, you're going to scream and yes, maybe I could have used a little more pain relief and been a bit more gentle, but then again that's what happens when you hang around the barrios getting drunk with the wrong crowd. Maybe this experience will make you think twice next time.'

Something like that anyway.

Later, during our time in Venezuela, we would speak to the brother of Carlos the Jackal, which was a pretty weird experience. Even so, it paled into insignificance compared to our visit to the main jail in Caracas.

We were told we could go into this prison and meet the inmates but cameras were not allowed inside. Now, this particular prison is under what they call Inmate Administration – the full meaning of which I was about to discover – but it was guarded on the outside by the Venezuelan military. So, for an initial fact-finding mission we went in without a camera.

First impressions? Waddling down the main corridor was a pig with the biggest pair of bollocks you've ever seen. Then there was a swimming pool – that's right, *a swimming pool* – with children playing in it. There were guys fitting braces, having their hair cut, having piercings, tattoos. There were women walking around, men and women kissing, the sounds of what can only be described as exuberant love-making coming from within cells. (And yes, in case you thought I'd wandered into a scene out of *Logan's Run* by mistake, there were actual cells in the prison, along with the swimming pool, the conjugal visits and the odd, well-endowed pig...)

Oh, and Christmas lights. Really. There were Christmas lights strung up everywhere. Caracas is constantly getting blackouts and now I knew why – all the electricity was being used to power the Christmas lights in this place. They had a huge snowman blowing snow out of his mouth into a ball the size of a car. It was the sort of thing you'd see in a big shopping centre back at home. That's where all the power was going.

So, obviously, I was walking around thinking, I *definitely* wanted to film inside here. Making *Extreme World* has taken me into some pretty grim prisons (see J is for John Mongrel) but this one was just totally surreal.

Next thing, we met Leo, who was the big boss of the prison. I asked him if we could get a camera into the jail. He shrugged and said, 'No problem, you get a camera in here, no problem.'

Lovely guy. Immaculately dressed. Though we never found out what he was imprisoned for, the fact that he was constantly surrounded by a kind of Praetorian Guard was proof of the enormous power he wielded within the prison. He showed us his cell, which was a perfectly nice cell. He had a big Bible on a lectern and pictures of his wife, who he'd met while inside. All in all, it was a pretty nice cell inside a nice, Christmas-decorated prison.

Except, the place had a smell.

And as I began seeing some of the less well-presented areas from which the smell emanated, I discovered it was the smell of crack. A few corridors away from the swimming pool and the Christmas lights and conjugal visits were tables – the kind you might see outside a pub on the A1. On them was more crack than I've ever seen, either before or since. Rocks and rocks and rocks of it.

The weird thing was, the crack was arranged in pretty little patterns, waves and swirls and Aztec shapes, patterns created by the dealers as a way of making their particular product look unique. A way of selling it, I suppose. It was almost beautiful. It would have been beautiful, perhaps, if they really had been crystals, the kind of stones little kids like collecting, rather than one of the most addictive and destructive substances on the planet.

So I was thinking, how on earth were we going to get the camera in? For a start, there was no way we were going to be able to use the usual camera we'd take on a job like this. What we decided to do was use a SLR camera, one that took a memory card on which we could fit about ten minutes' worth of film.

How to get it in? Leo told us to find a prostitute named Margarita, who not only worked the area outside the prison but came in and out on a regular basis. She would bring the camera in, and take it out for us. How was she going to do it? The answer was, don't ask.

As you can imagine, we were mega-dubious about the idea. Still, making the films, you end up putting yourself in situations where you simply have no choice but to trust somebody, and this was one of those times. Sure enough, when we left the prison that day we began asking people on the outside if they knew her. Me, Southan Morris the director, the cameraman Steve Lidgerwood and the female fixer, trawling around the square in search of a prostitute called Margarita.

At a beer vendor we struck gold.

'Ah, Margarita,' he said knowingly, and tipped us a wink before sending a kid off in search of the elusive Margarita.

We sat and drank beers, still wondering if we were making a huge mistake. A few minutes later the kid returned with a woman, I'd say in her mid-forties, bigger than most, you'd have to say, but a real character.

What's more she already knew exactly what we wanted.

We handed over about £3,000-worth of camera to her, with me thinking, 'I'm never seeing that again,' and Steve looking at me with a look in his eyes like, 'What the hell are you doing?' She smiled enigmatically, and that was it, she was gone.

We left, minus one camera, feeling like I don't know what: uncertain, stupid, like mugs who'd just been ripped off. We had no idea what we were supposed to do. Our only instructions were to come back five days later, when all would become clear.

So we did as we were told. We arranged a second fact-finding visit for five days' time, drove back to the prison, went to the beer vendor, asked for Margarita.

The guy shook his head. 'No, no, no idea where Margarita is' and we were about to begin shouting at each other, each one laying the blame at the other's feet, when the beer vendor grinned, 'The camera? Is it the camera you're after?'

Yes. Yes, it was the camera. Hope dawned as the beer vendor laughed and told us that Margarita had done as she was asked. She'd smuggled the camera into the prison.

We looked at one another. OK, right. That was a good start. We thanked the beer vendor and headed towards the prison gates.

Sure enough, when we met with Leo inside, he had our camera. We'd smuggled mics in and I had one taped to my chest as we joined him for what was to turn out to be a much more comprehensive and more eye-opening tour of the jail. Not just the holiday-camp side of it. Oh no. We were about to get the full warts-and-all experience.

We began by revisiting the good bits so we could film: Leo's private basketball court, the various satellite dishes up around the place, the library's brand-new DVDs, music everywhere.

Something else I noticed were strategically placed blocks of concrete. These, I realised, were armaments. Comfortable though the prison was – for the privileged inmates at least, we'll get to the less privileged prisoners in due course – it had been the scene of several riots, the most recent one lasting for thirty days. When the riot was eventually quelled by the army, troops found something like seventy kilograms of cocaine, rocket launchers, AK-47s, M-16s, and a lot of very dead people.

The concrete blocks were defensive and were strategically placed in order to form firing positions. If things kicked off in the prison, Leo and his men could retreat to an armed and well-defended inner sanctum. Clever guy. He had a fortress at the tip of his fingers. A fortified zone.

I managed to glean a little more information from Leo. Though he still didn't divulge why he was in prison, it became clear he was a member of a respected 'family', by which I took to mean 'crime family'. I asked him, 'Are you safer in here than you are outside?'

Leo looked around his well-appointed cell, with its shower, pictures of his wife and children, all of whom had been born while he was in prison, and all of whom appeared very well looked after, and he nodded. 'Yes, yes, probably safer in here.'

He also had a set of rules for inside the prison. The rules were very simple. You abide by the rules.

It was at this point that we started to hear about the 'other side of the prison'. The 'other side of the prison' was where you were sent if you broke the rules, Leo's rules. If you were caught stealing, for example, then you were sent to the 'other side of the prison'. You could smoke crack on the nice side of the prison but if you became addicted to it – and if you know anything about crack then you'll know how easy that can be – then you were sent to the 'other side of the prison'.

So, I suggested, let's go look at this 'other side of the prison'.

It was reached via a barred door guarded by men holding shotguns. We passed through the gate into a corridor that at first I thought was empty until I realised there were bodies slumped against the walls. Not dead bodies. Their eyes glowed in the dark as they stared up at me, muttering, whimpering. The only English words I could make out were, 'Help me. Please help me.'

And the stench – again it was the chemical smell of crack, of ether and kerosene. The walls were thick with sticky crack residue, as though somebody had come along and tried to paint them in brown tar. And then, just below that, the smell of shit – *rancid* human shit. The prisoners in this part of the jail simply hurled the faeces out of the windows where it baked in the sun. And, trust me, that's a smell you don't want to get used to.

With a hand over his mouth, Leo said, 'Why should I look after these people? Look at them, they are lost.'

Yeah, I thought, glancing at him, *but why was that?*

'Can you make it back to the good side of the prison?' I asked as we trod deeper into the groaning, pleading shadows.

Very rarely, was the answer, unless you get released – and getting released doesn't often happen. It took me a while to get my head around it, but the way it sounded was that if you were thrown in that part of the prison, that was it. Goodbye. *Adios.* You would more than likely never be seen or heard from again.

On the other side of the prison, Leo and his guards kept their weapons concealed on their person. That, I think, was one of Leo's 'rules'. But here on the other side – in hell's waiting room – the guns were taken out from their waistbands by his guards so they were visible to the poor souls within, warning of the consequences if they tried anything. Not that they looked capable of trying anything. These guys weren't so much living as subsisting. Surviving.

Everywhere I went were barely clothed men crouched in corners or lying in hammocks strung up between filthy walls, like giant cocooned moths. There were guys sleeping on the floors, men in crack comas. Their skin was like parchment or scorched leather. In the dark their eyes glowed and their mouths were black holes. They had no teeth. Deeper we went into the dark, stinking bowels of the jail and everywhere was the same murmuring and whimpering of skeletal men in rags, of crack addicts emaciated in every way: their bodies wrecked, their spirits sucked dry.

I met a Dutch guy who had been caught trying to take cocaine out of the country. Perhaps you've seen the movie *Midnight Express*? Here he was, living the film – only a far more terrible and horrifying version of it – for real. Twenty-one when he was caught, he'd been in the prison for eight years and was hopelessly addicted to crack, the spark of life behind his eyes tragically dim. He would die in here, I knew. I was sure of it.

I've rarely been more grateful to leave anywhere than

I was that prison that day. As we finally stepped out into the sunshine and fresh air, and went to the beer vendor in order to wait for Margarita, I wondered about Venezuela and the socialist dream of its leader Chavez. Whatever you thought of the prison's workings on the outside there was no doubt that they didn't even bother paying lip service to it on the inside – inside was a dictatorship presided over by Leo. And yet, it was Leo we had to thank for letting us see it, in order to show it to the outside world.

Leo and, thanks to her sterling work smuggling the camera in and then out again – and however she managed it, we certainly did not want to know – a prostitute called Margarita.

Q is for Quake

The fattest, healthiest dogs I've ever seen were in Haiti following the earthquake in 2010. The reason? Because there were so many bodies left lying around they were never short of anything to eat.

Arriving in the capital Port-au-Prince for an episode of *Extreme World*, we were greeted by scenes of utter devastation. The quake had struck on 12 January 2010, and a series of at least fifty-two aftershocks had continued until 24 January. The death toll was as high as 159,000, and an estimated 3 million people had been affected.

What quickly became clear was an almost total lack of aftercare. A whole bunch of medical staff had arrived and sewed people up, and then left. Nobody locally knew to remove the sutures, which became infected and led to people dying. Corpses were still buried beneath rubble, food for rats and dogs. We saw a pair of legs sticking out from the bottom of a building when we first arrived and a few weeks later they were still there. The only difference was that the trainers had gone, his jeans were no longer on his legs and the dogs had picked away most of the flesh from his legs.

In many cases the only solution was to pour petrol into the demolished houses and set fire to what was in there.

Everywhere you went there were internally displaced persons camps, hundreds and hundreds of makeshift tents, where abuse, rape and violence were rife and conditions were desperately insanitary. These were exactly the kind of conditions in which cholera thrives and, sure enough, a terrible situation had been considerably worsened by an outbreak.

For the film we joined a team of body collectors. This was like something out of the Dark Ages. Real 'bring out yer dead' stuff; the truck they were driving was piled high with bodies. When they come across an infected corpse, they plug up all the holes – upper and lower – with chlorine-soaked cotton wool in order to stop bacteria leaking out, because it's still infectious, even after you're dead. They then spray the entire body and surrounding area with chlorine from a plastic tank on their back, much like a rose sprayer. To make matters worse, a lack of understanding meant that people were unaware how the disease spread and they would often touch and sometimes kiss the corpses as they were being taken away. This meant that the body collectors would be back again in a few days' time.

Tom Watson was standing in for sound that day and we were halfway up a hillside collecting a body from a small village. As the corpse of an old lady was being sprayed by an over-zealous body collector, Tom got a shot of chlorine right in the face and was temporarily blinded. For a while, I was his 'eyes', and managed to lead him down the hill – 'left a bit, mate, right a bit' – until we reached the vehicle. It took us nearly an hour, with him in considerable discomfort, and accompanied by a man carrying the dead old lady the whole way.

Maybe we had a bit of a laugh about that later. And if that sounds harsh or inappropriate, you have to bear in mind that in a situation like Haiti, you either laugh or you cry. Sometimes both.

R is for the (thankfully) Rare Glimpses of Evil

People who do terrible things tend to believe their actions are justified. Whether it's for political or tribal reasons, or perhaps because they believe they're righting a wrong or feel let down by society, they usually see themselves as being in the right, the oppressed, not the oppressors; they want to look in the mirror and see a good guy.

Occasionally, though, you meet someone and you wonder just what on earth it is they see when they shave, because beyond personal gain or gratification there's nothing to justify their terrible wickedness. You wonder if they're just evil, through and through.

John Mongrel was one of these, without a doubt (see J is for John Mongrel), but there are a couple more worth mentioning.

The first, his name was Satan, and I met him during my trip to the Congo (see A is for 'Avez-Vous Le Boeuf?').

As I've already said, the war in the Democratic Republic of the Congo is funded through control of the mineral trade. Congo's most sought-after minerals are coltan and cassiterite. Coltan is used in our mobile phones, laptops, computer games and so forth. It stops the device from overheating when it's being charged up. Cassiterite is used in soldering.

When it's mined it leaves the Congo and is shipped to the Far East where it's smelted. By this point it's untraceable and will be sold on to electronics giants worldwide.

None of the huge electronics companies would ever admit it, of course, but given that the DRC has two-thirds of the world's coltan, it's highly likely some of the minerals used in their devices comes from DRC mines. I've got a mobile phone, of course, and I hate to think that by using it I'm helping to fund the kind of people who use rape and dismemberment as weapons, but having gone there I wonder: is it inevitable?

The mine owners are threatened and/or controlled by the militia who extract protection money or supplies of the mineral from the owners, who are themselves exploiting the workers. When you look at it that way, the chain of circumstances leading from the unmined mineral in the ground to the mobile phone currently in your pocket is potentially horrifying.

The trouble is, how do you tell? Once the minerals are melted down it's impossible to tell one bit from another. Has it come from legitimate suppliers in Australia or Brazil? Or is it stained with blood from the Congo?

The government hadn't wanted us to film at a mine, saying it was too dangerous, but we were insistent and eventually managed to wangle a UN escort to take us to a coltan and cassiterite mine fifty miles north of Goma.

We rendezvoused with our escort, who came with a Land Rover and an armoured personnel carrier, complete with mounted machine gun. Great, I thought, some decent protection – until it became apparent that the UN wanted us to drive ahead.

'That way we can protect you if we are ambushed,' said the commander. I looked at him as though he was mad. Perhaps there was some military reason why it wouldn't have been more sensible for our Toyota Land Cruiser to travel behind the protection, rather than in front of it, but I wasn't complaining – not until we came to where the road became a dirt track, and our UN escort turned around to go home, leaving us to continue alone on foot – an hour's hike down the hills towards the mine.

The dry but lushly green landscape rolled away from us in all directions. And it was to all intents and purposes an absolutely idyllic scene, until you took into account the fact that it was also home to militias, and the militias, though they didn't actually own the mines, would still benefit from them by setting up roadblocks and ambushes. The mine owners use women to carry the minerals and the militias demand 'taxes' using the threat of violence or rape or murder. Our hike took us right through the centre of militia country, with our UN protection an hour away. We were quite literally at the militias' mercy.

Arriving on a Sunday, we were greeted by a scene right out of the Stone Age. It was so hard to believe that this mineral was being used in phones and gadgets, and in some of the most advanced technology known to man, when it was being mined in such a primitive way: workers literally down on their hands and knees scrabbling at the dirt with picks and shovels and nothing else. I got down on my hands and knees had a go myself. Managed two minutes, tops. And though there weren't people standing over the workers with whips and guns or whatever, there might as well have been. After all, what was the difference between that and dying of starvation, which, it seemed to me, were the only two options available? I'd rather have the bullet personally. Rather that than the starvation.

The money skimmed off the mine went to fund guns and bullets – and thus to fund the militias who were responsible for some of the worst atrocities – the kind Denis Mukwege dealt with at the Panzi Hospital. I'd said that I wanted to look into the eyes of someone capable of those kind of atrocities, and when I met Satan, I did exactly that.

He told me he was Satan because he was fearless, like a hungry dog, just seven or eight years old when he first joined the militia, which was made up of 1,200 soldiers, up to 600 of which were child soldiers.

We sat opposite one another in a darkened room.

'Did you rape women?' I asked him.

Yes, he told me, raping happens very often. He had seen them happen and had personally participated when he was as young as thirteen, fourteen years old. He didn't feel happy about it, but he was in a group and all it needed was one person to start and the rest would join. He said he thinks a lot about what they did, but he can't turn back the clock.

This is war, he said. It happens.

There are two types of rape, he told me: raping in numbers or raping by order. Raping by order is where the commander orders you to do it. The aim is to destroy and you will follow the command instructions to the letter.

He showed little remorse about what he had done. He had the eyes of a killer with nothing to look forward to but a horrible future.

Though he was a self-confessed rapist, I could see the humanity within Satan. This was not the case when I met a man who, if he is to be believed, is one of the world's biggest mass murderers.

It was in India that I met him, for a film in the most recent series of *Extreme World*. Much of what we were doing in India focused on the problem of trafficking young people, mainly girls, for the sex industry, which is a huge problem. The official figure is around 30,000 girls who go missing every year, but we now think that figure is closer to 100,000. This is a country that spends more money on arms than the United States of America. They have a space programme. And yet every year almost 100,000 girls go missing from West Bengal and are forced into a life of prostitution. Some of the girls go willingly, without a full understanding of what it is they're going into. They think they're beginning jobs, taking on careers, that they'll be helping their families. One I spoke to left home to go to a job, was drugged on the way there and woke up tied to a bed where a guy had unprotected sex with her over and over again. A lot of people in that part of the world believe that having unprotected sex with a virgin will cure you of

Cassiterite and coltan mine deep in the heart of the Congo.

Hesco keeping us all safe in Musa Qala with 5 Scots, Herrick 8.

In water that was about to get deeper in so many ways, Peru.

Anti-narco squad. Me realising we are on our way back to the cocaine factory.

Above left and right: The cocaine factory: the chalk and the piscine.

Coca airport – before the controlled crash.

Thumbs up before our first take-off attempt.

Lucky Ducky to the rescue! Second take-off. Steve, our interpreter and Tim.

The Huaorani not too sure about our take-off plans.

The fabled green van, halfway up the Andes.

After all that effort and pollution, the end product: $2 million worth of cocaine paste.

With Little Man in Jamaica, a person I have huge respect for, despite his day job.

Above the clouds in the Andes.

Uber-producer Marta and me, El Salvador.

Top: With the IDF, Ni'Lin Israel.

Left: In the tunnel with a masked miner where three people die every week.

With the PRC just before entering the kitchen.

Israel. Aftermath of Operation Cast Lead.

Tear gas.

Tired, but still got it. But g[...]
what, is the question.

Chucho, El Salvador.
Leader of the Little
Psychopaths of Delgado.

A handshake with
the General PNG.

HIV and, well, I don't think you need to be a medical expert to work out what's going to happen in that situation.

We visited the police whose job it is to try and track down the girls, and were left in a state of shock at the resources they have to do such a gargantuan task. Walking into the team's headquarters, we found a tiny and cluttered room that looked like a local newspaper office in the 1970s. The few staff sitting on ancient office chairs had just three computers. That's *three* computers to deal with a problem on that scale. What chance did they have?

Sure enough, they were fighting a losing battle, as was starkly illustrated when, towards the end of our time in India I was able – thanks to the brilliant work of Tom Watson – to interview a sex trafficker.

We met him at a place called Osmanabad, famous for its brick kilns, and I sat down to talk to him.

Perhaps the first thing worth mentioning is how utterly blank he was. Gangsters I've spoken to in the past are often proud of their misdeeds, wearing them like a badge of honour, which of course is how they acquire status. I've spoken to other bad guys who seemed genuinely shameful for what they had done, and regretful for all the hurt they had caused people in the past. Satan, for example.

And then there were others – the likes of John Mongrel, for example – who just seemed so . . . *blank*.

The guy in the blue baseball cap, he was one of those. He talked about how the girls would be enticed into his operation and sold in batches at auction. They would be sold, either to madams for brothels or into households to become not just sex slaves but domestic slaves as well.

It was clear that we were talking about an awful lot of girls here. This guy was smartly dressed, had gold rings on his fingers, and I'd seen his car – it was a bloody good car for someone of his relatively tender years. He was making a lot of money.

But then, if he was trafficking so many girls, wasn't there a lot of police interest in his activities? Sure there was, he said, and if things got too hot – say if the police were look-ing for a girl then she would have to die. He would kill her.

Through the interpreter, I asked him how many girls he had personally killed.

He replied, and the interpreter began quietly weeping before gathering herself and telling me: 400 girls.

For a moment or so I looked into his eyes and he looked into mine and I knew that he was being deadly serious. I think he knew, too, that I was on the verge of flying at him. The rage I felt – I wanted to kill him.

But of course, I didn't. I pulled back, said something like, 'Get him out of my sight,' and he left, walking over to a side of the clearing where the interview was taking place and crying.

Maybe we should have restrained him. Tried to hand him in to the authorities.

Should we have let him go? I don't know. I didn't know then and I don't know now. Part of me thinks that if we had handed him over to the authorities then nothing would have happened. Part of me thinks we should have done something.

Hopefully, just by being there, we did.

S is for (I love the) Smell of Shit Pits in the Morning

'm sure you've heard of the Segway – a battery-powered, two-wheeled electric vehicle that was invented around the turn of the century by an American guy called Dean Kamen.

In December 2009 the Segway company was bought by a British multimillionaire called Jimi Heselden. Nine months later, Heselden died when the Segway he was riding plunged off a cliff. He was, by all accounts, one of the good guys: top bloke, a real family man. As well as leaving hundreds of millions to his family he was one of the country's biggest philanthropists, and among his charitable donations was £1.5 million to Help for Heroes and a whopping £23 million to help the poor and disadvantaged in his home city of Leeds.

Heselden knew what it was like to be broke. At the age of fifteen he left school and went to work down the mines, but lost his job following the miners' strike in the 1980s. With his redundancy money he began a sandblasting business. He then worked on developing a bit of kit that came to be known as the Hesco Bastion.

The Hesco Bastion is a collapsible wireframe. What they call a gabion. Very light and easy to transport, the Hesco is like a flat-packed concertina, which is unfolded then filled with concrete, sand, soil or gravel to be used as barriers or walls. It's been used a lot for flood-control applications, but by far its biggest application is military.

And in Iraq and Afghanistan they're absolutely everywhere. They stop small arms fire; they're more effective than sandbags against water, and at the right kind of thickness will even stop an RPG round. I don't know how many lives have been saved by Jimi Heselden's invention, but it must run into the thousands.

Where we come in, is on the second series on Afghanistan: *Return to Afghanistan*, where we joined up with five Scots at a town called Musa Qala.

To give you an idea of how fluid the situation was in Afghanistan, during the first series Musa Qala had been an Afghan Taliban stronghold. Now it was held by British troops and here was where we spent a month filming: days out on patrol, nights in the base, behind the walls of our Hesco Bastion. Some of the troops slept in tents; some, like us, in shelters made of Hesco. The advantage of Hesco? That it's safer than a tent. The disadvantages? Well, they're very hot for a start, and in a place like Afghanistan, where you're fighting the elements as well as the enemy, that made life uncomfortable.

In those days I was the worst snorer in the room. Not any more, funnily enough, but back then I honked like an express train racing towards a woman chained to the tracks. We had a motto: he who sleeps first, sleeps longest and that was largely due to the noise I made when I dropped off. Get to sleep before me and you stood a good chance of a good night's kip. But if I hit the land of nod ahead of you? Forget about it. What can I say? Sorry, lads.

The problem with being a snorer back then was that your mouth was open half the time, and one of the worst things about the air in Afghanistan is that you get what we used to call 'desert bogey', which is when the sand gets up your nose, sticks to the natural moisture in there and creates hardened shards of bogeys, like having shrapnel up your schnozz. Only it's not like if you have a cold and you can just blow it into a hanky to get rid of it and have done with it like you do at home. Oh no, desert bogies are like parasite bogies. They want to remain with the host organism, in this case you, and trying to blow them out will simply result in you either blowing to no avail or blowing too hard and filling a handkerchief with the entire lining of your nose. It really was that bad. It's the silica in the sand, is what it is. It's so sharp.

Afghanistan is the most hostile country on earth. I'm telling you, everything in Afghanistan either wants to bite you or kill you. The dust out there was slightly acidic. So say if you were scratched by thistles or grass, you had to be careful it didn't get infected with the dust because the dust would literally burn your body. You'd be screaming, like someone had rubbed lime into the wound.

It wasn't long after we'd arrived in camp that a terrible illness swept the base. An outbreak of diarrhoea and vomiting – informally referred to as D&V – gripped the camp within about twelve hours of it first being reported. According to medics it was a viral outbreak, which meant that the worst cases had to be quarantined. It would end up getting so bad that supplies of bog paper were exhausted and copies of *Nuts* magazine were being pressed into service and passed along a line of khazis that, once you got inside, were like a scene from Dante's vision of hell. It put our cameraman into quarantine and later, when I interviewed the commander Nick Calder who had also succumbed to the virus, he'd lost that much weight, he looked like a prisoner of war. I think I'm right in saying that he went down to around seven or eight stone.

About a day and a half after the first outbreak, news arrived that Afghan civilians had been hurt in a bomb blast and needed treatment. Six of them arrived and the already overstretched medical team made preparations to cope. There were children peppered with shrapnel and older men, also wounded, but doing their best to help those younger than themselves. A lack of female medics on the team caused problems because the female casualties wouldn't allow male doctors to operate on them. It was one of those times when the cultural differences became frustratingly apparent.

With our cameraman incapacitated due to his bout of D&V, producer Matt Bennett picked up the camera and we temporarily forgot about our own discomfort to film at the scene, fighting a mixture of sickness and shock, flinching at a rocket attack that came in the middle of it all.

With most of the wounded having received treatment, I watched a little girl eating a lollipop as one of the medics removed bits of shrapnel from her back. A Chinook arrived to transport the wounded back to the main hospital at Camp Bastion – my previous home.

Meanwhile, those rumblings I'd been feeling had got worse and worse and I soon realised that I was coming down with a case of the dreaded D&V. *Great.* That was just great.

Even worse was that night when I realised I needed to use the toilet, knowing I'd got the lerg. Knowing this was going to be no ordinary poo.

On went my head torch. The same head torch I later used to frighten off the beef hunters in the Congo (see A is for '*Avez-Vous Le Boeuf*?'). It has a red light and I flicked it on. The red light was so you couldn't easily be spotted by the enemy as you made your way about camp. It also had the effect of making everything seemed even more gruesome and brown and insanitary than it already was.

Some of the thunderboxes were marked for D&V only. There were rumours circulating about these particular cubicles. How revolting they were. I'd hoped never to have to use one. As I stumbled towards the line of toilets with all the classic symptoms of D&V I considered using one of the normal ones. After all, it wasn't like my particular germs were watermarked Ross Kemp. Who was going to know?

But no. A mixture of public spiritedness and fear of being caught out made me do the right thing. And in case you think I'm saying this for your benefit, I can assure you there's pictorial evidence of me using the right toilets. One of the benefits/drawbacks (delete as applicable) of travelling with a film crew is that virtually your every move is recorded. The opportunities for bullshit are very few and far between.

I stepped in, and it was beyond horrible. The red glow of my head torch made everything look a revolting purple colour and as I gingerly sat down I could see between my legs a seething mass of flies punctuated by tiny mushroom heads of white toilet paper. The Devil's own minestrone. I groaned with a mixture of pure revulsion and nausea as my bowels emptied and disturbed flies that billowed up towards my nether regions.

As if the general stench and attack of the flies wasn't enough, I heard vomiting from the cubicle next door and that was it. The straw that broke the camel's back. It made me retch too, instantly transforming me into a foul fluid-dispensing machine. Fair enough, it's called diarrhoea and vomiting for a reason, but you don't expect to be doing both at the same time.

I finished. Or at least I thought I'd finished. But the thing about the D&V was that just like the old ad for *Jaws II*, just when you thought it was safe to leave the thunderbox . . .

It struck again. I'd get a few paces clear away from the brown, flyblown swamp of shit, and suddenly, like a nightmare from which there was no escape, I had to return. It was as if the movement of walking somehow agitated all of that diarrhoea inside, and it had to get out again.

I wasn't the only one who realised that the best thing to do was simply stand in the cubicle (by this time I was wearing my T-shirt up over my nose, trousers down around my ankles, what a sight I must have been) and wiggle. I mean, literally, dance in the cubicle in order to try and enchant the diarrhoea from your body. A dance move that became known as the Musa Qala shuffle.

The viral outbreak lasted a few days, and anybody who caught it transformed almost instantly into an emaciated extra from *Bridge on the River Kwai*. I had a relatively benign dose. A medic pressed a couple of rehydration packets into my palm and told me to go to bed. I'd been up all night doing the Musa Qala shuffle so I needed no further encouragement. As I clambered gratefully into bed I thought of the poor sods whose job it was to empty the thunderboxes, dump it in what they call the shit pits, then set fire to it. What a job.

The whole burning-shit thing is common practice in Afghanistan. They have bags that you take a dump into then seal up and put in your backpack. Chemicals already present in the bag break down the excrement, and the idea is that when you get back to base you sling the whole thing into a shit pit where it gets burnt. It all works perfectly, assuming we're talking about one of your usual, healthy shits. Trouble is, the end result of a D&V attack is about as far from a normal, healthy shit as it's possible to imagine. It's liquid, after all. Slinging it on the shit pits was all well and good – after all, what else were you expected to do with it? The problem was it didn't burn the same way.

The other problem was that our Hesco shelter – the very Hesco shelter in which I was attempting to sleep off my thunderbox ordeal – was downwind of the shit pits. As I slept smoke had found its way through a gap in the hardcover. And when we woke up the next morning the smoke was in our eyes, our noses, our throats. When we stumbled outside and spat, desperately trying to get the revolting taste out of our mouths, the colour of the spit was brown, as though we'd been chewing tobacco.

Only we hadn't been chewing tobacco.

We'd spent the night asleep, blissfully unaware that we were inhaling the shit fumes of almost every man on the camp.

And maybe, just maybe, that was even worse than tear gas.

S is also for Soft Toys

S oft toys – I'm telling you, the harder they come, the more they love a cuddly toy. And in South and Central America, they go nuts for them.

This is women *and* men we're talking about. Walking around the Caracas prison (see P is for a Prostitute Called Margarita) in Venezuela, there were tons in the cells. The same goes for the El Salvador female prison, Susaltepeque, where we helped Chucho by getting him in to see his wife and baby (see C is for Carrier-Bag Cavity Search). Everywhere you looked, these huge cuddly toys.

Coming to the end of our time in El Salvador, we were on good terms with Chucho. His sister, Maria, had taken a shine to me. She'd bought me a soft toy (of course), smelling sweetly of scent. Not understanding the significance of this, I felt obliged to get her one in return (this one didn't smell sweetly of scent), which was a bit of a mistake given the high regard for soft toys in that part of the world. To her, it was practically a declaration of love. And because we'd been getting on so well we were invited to Chucho's house for a meal one night. Of course we agreed, off we went, and that evening, sitting round the table in Chucho's house, we tucked into a chicken meal, all very convivial.

Except when I looked at my chicken, it was still bloody and soft. And you know how it is with chicken – I mean, it's not like steak. You don't want to see blood. You want it cooked. In fact, if it comes to a choice between undercooked or overcooked chicken you go for the latter every time.

Trouble was, I'd been eating this chicken. Not the whole portion, thank God, but enough of it to know that things weren't going to go well. My stomach was already doing a bit of Vesuvius-like rumbling. Dishwasher-style churning.

Bad things were happening down below.

With me was Marta, on our very first job together, and I managed to catch her eye and tell her I needed to leave. She looked at me, and instantly knew something was wrong. Maybe it was my pallor or the way I was suddenly hunched forward in my seat, or maybe it was the sight of my terrified, beseeching eyes and the fact that I'd begun to sweat profusely – but she didn't need to ask if anything was wrong.

Chucho and family protested, but there was no way I could stay and I managed to juggle the need to be polite with the need to leave at once. I jumped in the car with Marta, and we began to make our way back into town.

So now I was sweating, arms across my stomach, cursing chicken – all chicken – as Marta drove as fast as she could, no doubt thanking her lucky stars that I'd got the bad bit of chicken and not her.

We arrived back at the hotel. By this time I was bursting. All I knew was that I had to get to a toilet because something was going to happen, and it was going to happen from both ends – probably at the same time.

'Can I get you anything?' called Marta as I hightailed it from the car.

'Anything to block me up,' I shouted back.

I reached the bathroom, tore down my kecks, plonked myself on the toilet and sure enough, just as the basement opened for business, the top floor did too. I shat into the toilet and puked in the bath.

It was some time later that I managed to gather myself, by which time Marta had arrived back with something medicinal that was passed gingerly through the bathroom door. A bottle of Pepto Bismol, bright pink in colour. It was the only thing she could find, she assured me, and as I was in a slightly delirious state I glugged it straight from the bottle, sat back on the toilet then lapsed into a drifting, semi-conscious doze.

How long I slept I'm not sure. All I remember is waking up very suddenly, on the floor next to the toilet, and knowing that the Pepto Bismol was about to make an urgent reappearance.

In the next instant I was redecorating the bathroom in a tasteful shade of Barbie pink. To this day, I still like my chicken so well done, it may as well be charcoal.

T is for a Totemic Tropical Take-Off

(. . . continued from N is for Never Walk Around the Back of a Helicopter)

So, to continue the tale. Most of our crew was at Coca airport, while poor old Tom was out there in the Ecuadorian jungle. Thinking about him, we recalled the story of Jim Elliot and the Operation Auca missionaries, who were speared to death by members of the Huaorani tribe – Tom's present hosts. Was Tom in similar danger, we wondered? How could we help him?

Straight away, we sprang into action. We went for a beer.

Now, because of the dramatic crash-landing at the airport, we were local celebrities, and found ourselves the centre of attention. In a bar that means you get drinks bought for you and, sure enough, before we knew it, the beers were being lined up. Why not, eh? We'd been through a near-death experience. Together the six of us had experienced the most terrifying thirty minutes of our lives and we were happy to toast our continued state of being alive.

In the meantime, we managed to organise a plane back to Yasuni. The only trouble was, it was such a small plane that not everybody would fit in it, plus Tom had all the kit.

So, to cut to the chase, and without going into all the ins and outs, what it meant was that Tom had to make his way back from Yasuni. If only we could get hold of Tom and tell him so . . .

Later we rolled up to the hotel, bit pissed, and tried to get a bed for the night.

'But you're not booked in tonight.'

'We've got nowhere else to stay. Please let us in . . .'

They relented, and at least we scored a bed for the night.

And then – more good news. I managed to get hold of Tom! On a BlackBerry of all things. In the few seconds I had before the intermittent signal died for good, I managed to tell him to get the hell out of Dodge and head back towards Coca, leaving behind some of our gear. That done, we retired, and I allowed myself to believe that the whole mess would be sorted out OK.

At first light we dragged our tired and slightly hung-over carcasses back to the airport, where we were greeted by the plane that was to take us to Yasuni.

This thing – well – it was a flying bucket. I mean, officially it was a Cessna, but it looked more like someone had taken a 1970s Sprite caravan and nailed a couple of planks of wood to the roof and put a propeller on the front for a laugh. Once bright yellow, it had faded, gone to seed, so it was now a dull, brown, mildewy colour.

We assembled to board the flying caravan: me, Steve Lidgerwood the cameraman, Tim Watts the soundman and the translator. And Southan? The weight restrictions in the flying caravan meant our illustrious director got to stay at

Coca, where all he had to do was cool his heels before our flight to Quito, the capital of Ecuador.

(The onward flight from Quito to Lima, by the way – we had to get that or face a four-day wait until the next one, which was not an option. So if all this sounds like a desperate race against time with members of the crew and bits of kit in various different places in Ecuador, then, yes, that's precisely what it was.)

Our pilot turned up. You remember Frank Cannon, the detective from *Cannon*? Big guy? Him and our pilot were separated at birth.

We boarded, and once inside I became aware that the pilot had more than the usual array of crosses, Madonnas and St Christophers. South Americans are a religious bunch at the best of times but this guy really took the biscuit. What's more, it soon became clear that his faith was practically the only thing keeping the plane airborne.

Me, I've always loved flying. However the fact that planes stay up in the air defies the laws of physics. There are several theories as to why aeroplanes work. There should be one theory, am I right? But no, there are *several*. What's more, none can explain exactly why, when you drive a winged vehicle at the right speed, it will take off and remain in the sky. There is, in short, a certain degree of magic involved. Or perhaps input from some higher power.

Either way, we got up, and once up, our pilot was constantly trimming the aircraft as he spoke to the translator, who told us that the air was thin. The way he explained it was that as the day wore on, the air would only get thinner, so we had to make our stop-off in Yasuni quick, or risk not being able to take off again that day. (And any delay in take-off meant missing our onward flight to Lima.)

On a strip not much longer than the average hopscotch grid, we managed to land. We disembarked and I met Moi Enomenga, a member of the Huaorani tribe who took me downriver in order to show me the effect of oil drilling on his tribe, and then we went hunting with spears and blowpipes. A wonderful morning.

But perhaps a bit lengthy, because by the time it came to leave, our pilot was not a happy man. With good reason, as it turned out. Sweating, he urged us to board the flying caravan and we clambered aboard. With less time to pack and get ourselves sorted we were jammed into the cabin, and I had the feet of a camera tripod pressing into the small of my back, acutely aware how sharp they are. How I could easily end up impaled on them.

Meanwhile, the pilot was evidently shitting himself. A dark sweat stain had appeared on the orange polo shirt he wore, and he was fingering his religious icons like a genie might appear. His fear was infectious and pretty soon we were all shitting ourselves, too, as he taxied to the very beginning of the landing strip – the so, so short landing strip – taking the plane so far back it was actually off the end of the strip.

I was pushed right to the front with the sharp legs of the tripod in my back. In the back was soundman Tim, all six foot four of him, the translator and Steve, who as the pilot began to rev the engine, suddenly delved into his pocket and yanked out a small plastic duck.

'Boys, boys, boys,' he yelled above the roar of the engine, 'everyone have a stroke of lucky ducky.'

Any other time or place I'd have laughed and so would Tim, but not right now. We all had a stroke of lucky duck. All except the pilot, who was touching all his Madonnas and St Christophers, and leaning over the control like a man possessed as the plane began to taxi forward, slow at first but gathering pace as we moved up the runway.

The dwelling used by Moi Enomenga and his family was about halfway down the runway and they stood waving us off. I distinctly remember passing them and waving back, seeing the looks on their faces, as if to say, 'You're going to die . . .'

I faced front, watched the line of trees at the end of the runway getting closer and closer, the nose of the plane refusing to rise.

Somebody shouted, '*Come on*,' and I realised it was me.

The noise of the engine had reached an ear-splitting pitch, the line of trees getting closer and closer.

'Lucky duck, lucky duck, lucky duck!' we were shouting.

'*Come on!*'

But to no avail. All we saw was the green of the approaching trees and I'm no pilot but even I knew that the nose should have been lifting. In other words: by now we should have been seeing blue, not green.

Sure enough, the pilot's hands were a blur as he shut everything down and leaned forward on the stick, the flying caravan lurching to a halt just a few feet shy of the treeline.

We looked at each other, gulping, as the pilot turned the plane around and we began taxiing back to the start point. This was serious now. I mean, even *more* serious. Each moment we wasted the air got thinner and our chances of actually making it off the ground decreased. I was thinking of Southan back at Coca, probably enjoying a glass of cold beer right now. Thinking of Tom making his way back through the jungle to Coca to catch our onward flight.

As we passed Moi and his family, I pulled a face at them, like, 'OK, let's try this again.' They weren't waving at us any more. They were doing the Huaorani equivalent of crossing themselves.

'Another stroke of lucky duck,' insisted Steve, and five sweating blokes gave lucky duck a stroke.

'Come on, lucky duck,' we were shouting, as the pilot gunned the throttle, 'come on lucky duck.'

We began taxiing again. Faster now. Every man inside willing on the plane with mind, body and soul. Suddenly the plane was no longer a crappy old Sprite caravan, it was a plucky Cessna powered by lucky duck.

'Lucky duck, lucky duck, lucky duck!' we were chanting as the plane gathered speed.

Back past Moi and his family, now a blur.

'Lucky duck, lucky duck, lucky duck!'

The treeline approached. The noise of the engine was unbearable. By now we were past the point where we'd pulled up last time but there was no stopping now and the nose was – *at last* – lifting.

'Lucky duck! Lucky duck! Lucky duck!'

And the front wheels had left the landing strip, and at last I could see a bit of blue – as I gripped the dashboard so hard I thought I was going to leave my fingernails behind and the plane climbed just enough to scrape the tops of the trees and get us airborne.

As close as it gets.

But the ordeal was still not at an end, because we got back to Coca, amazingly, without incident, apart from the fact that it appeared as if we had carried half the Amazon rainforest back with us in the plane's undercarriage. We grabbed our stuff off the plucky Cessna and loaded it on to the big, safe-looking jet that would take us to Quito, but . . .

There was still no sign of Tom.

And we never leave a man behind. I mean, I know it sounds gung ho, like something you hear in Vietnam movies, but it's true and it's a mantra you live by making our films: nobody gets left behind.

By now the passengers had boarded the jet and it was us lot who were last on. But there was still no sign of our producer.

And then came a call. It was Tom saying, 'I'm just off the boat . . .'

We began to take our time getting into our seats, 'Oh, I'm having such trouble with this overhead locker,' while keeping one eye on the open door of the aircraft, wondering how long it would take him to get across Coca to the airport, through the terminal and on to the plane.

Another call from Tom. 'I'm in a taxi, hold the plane.'

Thinking, *We'll do our best, mate, we'll do our best.*

But it quickly became apparent that the crew were getting ready to shut the doors and take off. Seeing us still dithering with overhead lockers and stuff, stewardesses were closing in on our position, beginning to insist that we remain in our seats.

Come on, Ross, I thought. You're a fucking actor. *Act.*

'Excuse me,' I said suddenly, and stood. 'I'm going to have to get off the plane. I've got to use the toilet.'

She didn't quite understand what I meant, but she knew what I was intending to do and her mouth dropped open.

'No,' she said, waving me back to my seat. 'Please, sit.'

Believe you me, I'm used to dealing with tough women and, not to be intimidated, I continued up the central aisle.

'No, no,' I insisted, 'I *really* need the toilet.'

I made it to the open door, the stewardess on my tail, and for a moment or so we tussled, half in, half out of the aircraft. She was jabbering at me in Spanish while I was doing an acting-class improvisation of a man with rabies/ malaria/the shits, whatever, just doing anything I could, short of throwing myself from the top of the gantry and to the apron below, to stall take-off.

And then I saw him: Tom, speeding through the terminal, running like his life depended on it, then streaking out on to the tarmac and bounding up the steps towards us.

Immediately I recovered from my rabies/malaria/poo-related problem and at the same time the stewardess let go of me, suddenly realising exactly what had been going on, as an out-of-breath and heavily perspiring Tom presented his ticket and we both took our seats, ready for our journey to Quito.

Thank God it was only a two-hour flight. Let me tell you, I was not the most popular passenger on board.

U is for Underground Tunnels

The Erez Crossing between Israel and Gaza is one of the most heavily fortified border crossings in the world. All IDF troops stare at you suspiciously, it's in their DNA, but on the Erez Crossing you can expect to be eyed with even more suspicion than usual.

In fairness, it's with good reason. In 2004, Reem al-Riyashi, a twenty-two-year-old Palestinian mother of two, became the first female Hamas suicide bomber when she managed to infiltrate the Erez inspection hall and detonated an explosive device. It killed three soldiers and a civilian employee and injured ten, including four Palestinians.

After the attack a video emerged that showed her wearing combat fatigues, saying that since the age of thirteen she'd dreamt of turning 'my body into deadly shrapnel against the Zionists'.

A year later, another woman, Wafa al Bass, was stopped before she could detonate the twenty-two-pound bomb she had strapped to her leg. She was released from prison in 2011 as part of a prisoner exchange and was last heard urging more Palestinians to become martyrs.

So if the IDF troops at the Erez Crossing were suspicious when we used it, first to pass from Israel into the Gaza Strip and then back again, well, we'll forgive them. They had good reason.

Going through the crossing from Israel was like entering a different world, like driving into the Congo from Rwanda (see A is for '*Avez-Vous Le Boeuf?*'). Israel is rich, massively developed and very high-tech. We left it behind as we entered the terminal, carrying our gear. If you can cast your mind back to the scene in *Dr No* where Bond is captured then disinfected by the baddie's henchmen, well, it felt similar to that. Our kit was thoroughly searched and in what I can only describe as looking like a decompression chamber we were 'spun' and checked for weapons and explosives.

In the chamber, stony-faced IDF troops stood on the safe side of protection detective glass. This glass is so thick it will withstand bullets and explosives. They talk to you via an intercom system. Below your feet is a trench of sorts. This is in the event of explosives being detonated in the 'decompression chamber'. The below-floor area absorbs much of the blast; the walls and glass protect the guards. Basically, if you set off a bomb in this room the only person to die would be you.

Two weeks later, after our adventures in the Gaza Strip (see also B is for Be Careful Where You . . .) we returned to Israel, again via the Erez Crossing.

As is often the case, the security coming back to Israel was far tighter than it had been on the way out. This time we were spun, then spun and spun again, but although certain members of our party (naming no names, Tom Watson) were bringing back souvenirs, it was yours truly who got picked on by the IDF guards. Maybe they didn't like my face. Maybe they were *EastEnders* fans and were still cross about what happened to Tiffany.

Who knows? Either way, I was taken into a separate room, which unlike the decompression chamber, had just one door in and out, the most bombproof room I've ever seen. Even the window through which the IDF troops viewed me seemed thicker than the protective glass in the other parts of the terminal.

This, in other words, was where they brought you when they suspected you of being a suicide bomber.

'Sit,' I was told. So I did, taking a seat on a plastic pub-style chair that had been placed in the centre of the inspection chamber.

I squinted at the inspection-chamber window, through which the guards regarded me implacably, patiently awaiting my next orders. I was nervous, but not *that* nervous, thinking that this was more than likely a show of strength. The IDF troops knew we'd been making a documentary and they knew that it would entail talking to members of Hamas – terrorists, in other words. We were almost certain we'd been under surveillance during our time in the Gaza, so this, perhaps, was a way of putting us in our place.

So it came as no surprise that there was one final hurdle to jump. What did come as a surprise was what happened next.

'Take off your clothes, please,' the voice said. Disembodied and metallic. And maybe because it was so disembodied and metallic-sounding, I didn't quite get what they meant.

'I'm sorry?' I said, cupping my ear.

'Take off your clothes.'

'You're not serious.'

A slight pursing of the lips indicated that he was deadly serious, that he had never been more serious about anything in his life.

'Take off your clothes,' he repeated, in the tones of someone who was not prepared to give the order a third time.

I stood, shaking my head at them as if to say, 'Is this really necessary?' and then, because I thought that the whole thing was a bit of a pisstake decided to take the piss back.

I began whistling the music, you know – the stripper music. And started to do the proper burlesque unbuttoning. 'You want to see me take my clothes off, do you?' I jeered.

But with a shake of the head, as if to say 'enough is enough', my interrogator stopped me.

Shame, he was about to see a proper Gaza Strip.

Anyway, rewind, back to our initial trip through the Erez Crossing, when we passed from high-tech Israel into the Gaza Strip, which was Stone Age in comparison. Rubble age.

The area on the other side of the crossing had been comprehensively bombed by the Israelis during Operation

Cast Lead in 2008–2009. A year later, here we were. Hamas in control of Gaza, and me trudging across a half-mile wasteland that constituted a no-man's-land between Israel and Gaza, with derelict buildings either side of me – imagine a bombed-out Dover port – until I came to the Palestinian checkpoint.

Here there was no spinning. No decompression chamber. There were just some guys going through our stuff to make sure we had no booze or porn before waving us on our way.

And that was it. That was our experience with the Erez Crossing. Once it had been a busy thoroughfare, taking supplies to and from Israel and Gaza. Now, though, it was a virtual wasteland.

So where was Gaza getting its supplies? The answer – or at least some of the answer – lies in Rafah. So there we went.

In our Nissan van – deliberately low-key so as to avoid interest from kidnappers – we drove out of Gaza City, where everywhere I looked I saw destruction left over from Operation Cast Lead, and set off for the southern town of Rafah, which was rumoured to be the capital of the black market in the Gaza Strip.

Rafah is on a closed border with Egypt. It looks like a large encampment of tents and tarpaulins but it is in fact the heart of the smuggling operation in Gaza. Smugglers pay tax to Hamas to keep more than 1,200 tunnels open. It's basically state-sanctioned smuggling, which explained the presence of Hamas officials there for my visit. It's also a very dangerous place to be. On average three tunnel workers are killed each week either by attacks by Israel or Egypt or, more likely, by the roofs collapsing.

So guess who was going to go down?

'Are you going to go down?' said an evidently incredulous Ahmed Yousef, the Deputy Foreign Minister of the Hamas government.

'Yes, I'm going to go down,' I told him.

'You have enough courage to go down?'

'I hope so,' I told him.

'It will be something you'll never forget.'

He'd turn out to be right about that.

I sat on what looked like a seat taken from a child's swing and repurposed as a lift down into the mineshaft. We'd been filming guys coming up and down this particular list and they were scrawny young lads and, in case you hadn't noticed, I'm not a scrawny young lad. I perched my arse on this seat, this kiddy seat nicked from a playground with some bolt holes in it and clamps and wire fixing it to the winch, and as I swung above the shaft I looked down. What immediately struck me was how badly constructed it was.

Before I could voice any concerns, they began to lower me down. It slipped and I left part of my fingernails in the sides of the shaft. There was no going back.

The cameraman Andy had gone down ahead of me and together we ventured along the tunnel. It was hot, very hot, and the further we got into the tunnel the narrower it became, the more the ceiling got lower, and the more the temperature rose. Not only that, but I began to see cracks in the tunnel walls. On more than one occasion clay simply fell from the tunnel as I passed. There were beams, supposedly holding the place up, that were cracked and evidently were on the very point of giving away completely.

By now I was beneath the border with Egypt so where was I expecting to end up? Well, I suppose, Egypt. And very much looking forward to reaching daylight. No way was I coming back along this tunnel. It was a cave-in waiting to happen. Anybody who used it needed their head testing as far as I was concerned. With 1,200 channels to choose from, I was going to make sure I chose a safer one for the return journey.

But there was no sign of daylight. We rounded a corner fervently hoping to be greeted by a friendly shaft of daylight. Instead what I saw made my heart drop. We had reached the end of the tunnel, but there was no daylight.

There was no exit.

They were still digging it.

What had greeted me was the sides of the tunnel held up by scaffolding and wooden beams, all of which looked like they'd seen better days, and the bare feet of the kid digging it. He was literally burrowing away at the face as we watched. He was using a trowel. The sort that old ladies in the Home Counties use in their gardens. *A trowel.*

OK, hold it together, Ross.

I'm not claustrophobic. But it was one of those situations where I had to remind myself of the fact. Air is pumped into the tunnels but there's not much of it. I was sweating like never before, being careful to maintain my breathing and successfully (thank God) controlling a rising sense of panic, because all of my fantasies about finding a safer tunnel back had turned out to be exactly that – fantasies. I was going back along this subterranean passage whether I liked it or not.

I turned and did my piece to camera. I saw that Andy the cameraman had gone a shade of white. He looked like I felt.

But we managed to keep it together and made our way back along the tunnel.

There was a rumour that all sorts of stuff came back along these tunnels. Weapons? When I had asked that one I was greeted with a shrug that told me all I needed to know, but even so I hardly bothered asking whether or not it was true that they had tried to bring a lion back through the tunnels for the Gaza zoo. Rumour had it the tranquillised lion had woken up halfway back and mauled a couple of the smugglers to death.

So now we started to make our way back. Was I imagining it or were there even more bits of tunnel crumbling around us as we scuttled back towards the entrance shaft?

By now Andy had stopped filming as we focused on getting the hell out of Dodge, and at the bottom of the shaft we signalled for the kiddy seat, strapped him into it and he was winched above ground in order to get footage of me emerging from the mineshaft.

Which is what happened. And if you watch the film, what you see is a very sweaty and slightly shaken Ross Kemp appear from the opening of the mine. What you didn't see is what had happened before that, for as I watched Andy being winched to safety there came a rumbling sound from the passage behind me. It was followed by screaming and shouting and then running feet as two mineworkers came belting back towards me pursued by a huge cloud of grit and sand that quickly enveloped me and bloomed upwards towards those waiting for us up top.

Amid the shouts in Arabic I heard my name being called.

'You all right, Ross?'

'Yeah, mate, I'm fine, thanks,'

In the sense that I hadn't been buried alive in the Gaza smuggling tunnel, yes, I was all right. In the sense that I'd had the fright of my life? Not so all right.

It turned out that there had been a partial collapse. That it had taken place at some point halfway between the shaft and the mine face. A spot where three or four minutes earlier Andy and I had been scuttling back to safety was now submerged in sand and earth.

A close shave. *Very* close shave.

V is for a Very Dangerous Place to Go for a Run

Staying in Dili, the capital of East Timor, for *Gangs* (see E is for Everything You Always Wanted to Know About Tear Gas Part II), I used to go for a run along the beach every day. This was partly thanks to a technical cock-up, which, without going into the gory detail, meant that we were stuck there for an extra two weeks (and there are worse places) waiting for the right kind of film stock to turn up, and partly because the ocean was beautiful and there's nothing I like better than beach running. Do it at home, do it abroad when I can. Awesome.

Anyway, cut to the chase. Every morning I took a run along the beach not far from the hotel, and each morning what I used to do was finish by a little bay at the end of the beach, where there was a pool in which I'd rinse off.

Well, I say 'rinse off'. Taking advantage of the fact that it was deserted, I'd lie and wallow for a while, watching bamboo moving lazily on the surface of the water, relaxing after my run. The heat was absolutely tropical and wherever you went in Dili was the ever-present threat of violence, so this pool at the end of my run was like a little sanctuary, a relaxing cool-down away from it all. To my right were locals enjoying the beach, to my left GNR guys doing weights. Why on earth weren't they coming to this beautiful beach, I wondered, but was more than happy to be left in splendid isolation. More fool them for missing such a gorgeous spot. It certainly didn't stop me enjoying my morning ritual.

Until our fixer, Auricio, put me straight. Wide-eyed, he told me to stay well clear of that bit of the beach.

'Why?' I said.

'You know what they call that beach?'

I shook my head, certain I was about to find out.

'Snake Beach,' he told me.

'Snake Beach?'

Turned out 'Snake Beach' was where East Timor's deadly sea snakes went to reproduce.

My cool-down pool? It was a snake shag palace. And that seaweed I'd been watching gently swish in the current? You've got it. They were East Timor's deadly sea snakes, which can kill you with one bite.

I gave Snake Beach a miss after that.

W is for a trip to the White House

One of the most eye-opening films I've made was an episode of *Gangs* in which we travelled to South Africa to find out more about the Numbers, a terrifying gang working out of the hellish Pollsmoor Prison in Cape Town.

Though the Numbers are a prison-based outfit, they have affiliations with the outside, and in particular Cape Town's Cape Flats. A ramshackle warren of dilapidated housing blocks, rundown shanty shacks and tents, the Cape Flats is home to around 2 million South Africans – 2 million South Africans living in absolute grinding poverty.

Now, as I discovered on my travels, wherever you find grinding poverty you find gangs, and Cape Flats is no different. I was told there are approximately 200 gangs living in the twenty-five by eighteen-kilometre area of Cape Flats and I could believe it. Everywhere I looked was gang graffiti. Groups of young men in baseball caps and basketball shorts loped around the streets or hung out on corners, wearing that unmisteakable gang look you see almost everywhere in the world. Elsewhere it's copied, perhaps, by impressionable young minds sold on the idea of gang cool. But here there was no doubt this was the true street life. This was reality.

Accordingly the threat of violence hung in the air, so easily triggered by looking the wrong way at the wrong person, or members of one gang stepping – deliberately or accidentally, it didn't matter – into the territory of another. The hundreds of gangs of the Cape Flats live in close proximity, often separated by a single street. Violent territorial disputes weren't just commonplace, they were daily.

The Cape Flats gangs began their affiliations to the Numbers during the 1980s, when the introduction of harder drugs into the drug food chain had a major impact on the trade and the relative prosperity of those now coming in to prison.

These new Cape Flats gangsters had no desire to be systematically raped as 'wyfies' by members of the Numbers in Pollsmoor – funnily enough – and having the money to buy themselves out of it, promptly did so. As a result they became *de facto* members of the Pollsmoor gang and once released took Numbers traditions and ideology with them back to the Flats. As far as South Africa's gang culture was concerned, Pollsmoor was its beating corrupted heart. I've talked about my visit there (see J is for John Mongrel) but suffice to say that it fully deserves its place in my A–Z of Hell.

Back in the Cape Flats, and I began hearing more about some of the gangs. The Sexy Boys, the Hard Livings, the Dixies, the Ghetto Boys and, of course, the two biggest: the Firm and the Americans.

It was in the Cape Flats that I met Kevin, a member of the Americans gang who took me to meet some fellow gang members.

The base? Where else would the Americans meet but at the White House? Not nearly as salubrious as its Washington namesake, the Cape Flats White House was a low timber-built building with a corrugated-iron roof that had been painted white. Inside it were low ceilings, a Stars & Stripes flag hanging on the wall, various US-style souvenirs and some very careworn seating.

No Oval Office, though, as far as I can remember. Instead, there was a group of Americans gang members who were . . . well, what's a polite way of saying this? Already in 'an advanced state of refreshment', perhaps?

Why? They were smoking crystal meth, which in Cape Town is known as tik. Crystal meth use in South Africa has exploded during the past decade. Until around 2003, the drug was virtually unknown, now it's Cape Town's main hard drug. What users do – indeed, what my new mates in the White House were doing – is take it by removing the metal and filament parts from a light bulb then heating the glass and stretching it out to form a pipe. Into the pipe goes the crystal meth, which looks like crushed glass and in fact is often called glass for that very reason. The user heats up the pipe, inhales the smoke and that's it, job done, one crystal meth hit.

Now, the crystal meth high is a big 'up' high, so what my guys were doing was levelling off with a mix of marijuana and the sedative Mandrax. They packed the neck of a broken beer bottle with marijuana and crushed-up Mandrax pills, mixed the whole lot together, set it alight and inhaled.

So in one toke, crystal meth – *up*.

In the next toke, Mandrax/marijuana – *down*.

I mean, Christ only knows how that felt – it must have been like going up and down Canary Wharf in a broken lift for hours on end. *Up. Down. Up. Down.*

And God knows how they did it, but some of the gang members were actually able to hold a conversation in this state and we began the interview.

It was a tiny room. A fug of smoke literally hung in the air, and though it doesn't show up so well on the film, the whole time it felt like I was squinting at the gang members through a layer of fog. It also meant that every time I opened my mouth to speak I was getting a generous dose of secondary smoke. That oh-so intoxicating mix of crystal meth, marijuana and Mandrax. You got it, I was getting accidentally shitfaced.

Still, the interview went on.

One of the main topics of conversation was the ethnicity of the gang members. The Americans were not white but nor were they black. They were what's known in South Africa as Cape Coloureds, which in that particular society is at the bottom of the ladder. Or so they thought. In their eyes was the resentment of ages. I asked them what they thought the future held for them and they had no answer. Watching them squabble over modified light bulbs and broken beer bottles used as drug receptacles, you couldn't help but think their options were a little on the limited side.

Some of the gang talked fluidly, tongues loosened by the tik. Others sat, almost comatose, watching me. One in particular was a budgerigar, and . . .

Wait a second – a budgerigar?

I blinked to try and clear my head. You've got to bear in mind that these guys were hardened, habitual crystal meth users.

Me? I had no tolerance for this stuff. Even the relatively tiny amount I was inhaling was getting me off my face.

Also bear in mind that even though the interview lasts about five minutes onscreen, we did the audience a favour and cut out hours' worth of the gang members smoking drugs, squabbling over drugs, surfing hits and talking absolute gibberish. In order to get the five minutes of usable film you see onscreen I was in the White House for three hours. The soundman, Jeff Hodd, and cameraman, Craig Matthew, took breaks and went outside, so they weren't so badly affected. Me, on the other hand . . .

Much later, when we reviewed the footage we realised that by the end of the sessions the gang's members really were talking gibberish. Complete nonsense.

At the time, though, I didn't realise. That's because I was talking gibberish too. Not only that, but the gang members were continuing to morph into birds. In some cases it was an improvement, but even so, as far I was concerned it wasn't a welcome development. Looking across the room I could see Jeff and Craig looking unwell, too. No doubt about it, it was time to beat a retreat, so we stopped filming and thanked the guys for their time.

I got to my feet on unsteady legs and we staggered to the door and out into the fresh air and sunshine. Outside we tried to do a piece to camera but it was a complete non-starter and we never used it. Instead there's a shot of me staggering away from the White House. Have a look at it. I got into the car, returned to the hotel at 12.30 p.m., scoffed scones and jam, drank a litre of water then went to bed – and wasn't seen again for twenty-four hours.

X is for Extremely Bloody Cold

In a lot of the places I've travelled to, heat was the problem. And when I think of the hottest I've ever been I think of that night in the Congo or in the tunnels in the Gaza Strip.

But when I think of the coldest I've ever been, what comes to mind is Afghanistan, funnily enough, when I swear I nearly got hypothermia. We were with the Royal Anglian and went out with B Company on what turned out to be a sixteen-hour yomp through some of the toughest territory the country has to offer – and take it from me, Afghanistan has some very tough territory to offer. Because you're wearing so much gear – your helmet, your body armour, your backpack – you sweat like I don't know what, so as night fell and it began to get cold our temperatures plummeted. Even so, we needed to rest so we lay down in a maize field, trying to forget that the Afghans fertilise their fields with their own faeces, and began to feel our sweat-soaked clothes chill our flesh.

And we started to get cold. I mean, *really* cold. Afghanistan has the most diverse temperatures and here we were at the real bottom end of it. The lot of us began to shiver violently in the shit-smelling maize field. We wanted to sleep but falling asleep was dangerous because when you're that cold you can slip into a coma.

Even so – and even shivering so hard in my clothes, I felt myself begin to doze . . .

Kick.

A boot right in the side woke me up. Squaddies were going round kicking us to make sure we stayed awake.

Starting to feel sleepy . . .

Kick.

Believe me, a squaddie boot in the ribs is better than any alarm clock.

Beginning to doze . . .

Kick.

After a while we gathered ourselves and took off again and I reflected that in war you can have all the high-tech gear you want, but at the end of the day what really matters is squaddies kicking you awake. It's the guys on the ground looking out for each other that really counts.

Y is for You Don't Want to Do That, Mate

Our time in the Gaza Strip had been memorable for all kinds of reasons, not least our narrow brush with death at the PRC hideout in Nigella's kitchen (see B is for Be Careful Where You . . . Oops, Too Late). Little did we know there was more to come.

It was our last day, but as we headed for the border we received a call from a military faction called the al Nasser Brigade, the military wing of the Popular Resistance Committee. They'd requested a meeting with us.

We wondered why. The al Nasser Brigade claimed responsibility for bombings in Israel, but apart from that and knowing that they'd been formed in 2000 and included ex-members of Hamas and Fatah, we knew nothing about them and had no idea what they wanted. Kidnapping? Trap? Loads of possibilities crossed our minds – including the one that we decided to go with: that they just wanted to put forward their side of the story.

The day came and we were greeted by two guys carrying AK-47s before our little Nissan van was taken on a magical mystery tour that ended with us stopping at the side of a road. A number of masked men with RPGs met us then ushered us out of the car and across some dry land towards what looked like a shaded area that turned out to be an orchard. Again, my greatest concern was not necessarily what these guys might do to us, but what the eyes in the sky might be seeing and what the Israeli response might therefore be.

And there in the orchard was a suicide bomber.

And let me tell you, there was no doubt whatsoever that he was a suicide bomber. He wore a balaclava, and a vest full of explosives. In his hand he held a little trigger that was wired to the vest – and he was oddly detached. Yet all the while maintaining a great dignity, which was no mean feat considering that he wore a suicide vest packed with explosives.

His comrades pointed a video camera his way and I realised why we'd been brought here. It was to witness the making of a martyr video.

'I am a living martyr, committed to this task to satisfy God, for my country . . .'

I couldn't help but notice that he was fiddling with his trigger as he spoke. And then, when he'd finished the video and I begin interviewing him, he was still fiddling with the trigger.

He was a university graduate, he told me, with his finger on the trigger, and his family had been killed. My eyes went from his hand to the explosives. Everything seemed to be attached.

I asked him if what he was doing would increase or

decrease violence. He seemed quite exasperated as he answered. 'They are attacking my country, and I must defend it in any way possible.'

He fiddled with the trigger.

Did he know there were Israelis who wanted peace? I asked him.

'Of course I support peace, but my country is occupied,' he told me. 'War brings war. Peace brings peace.'

I have to say that I breathed a sigh of relief when the interview finally ended and, with half an eye on the trigger, I thanked him and left, not at all sad to be getting back to the relative safety of the car. His detachment had been unsettling.

I had little doubt that, given the chance, he would achieve his goal.

Z is for Zebra Crossings (or whatever the equivalent is) in Venezuela

We were in Venezuela for the second series of *Extreme World*, which just so happened to be the first series produced by my new production company Freshwater, so holds a special place in my heart.

Not that this has anything to do with using zebra crossings in Venezuela, you understand. I just thought I'd mention it. No, the point about not using zebra crossings in Venezuela is that Venezuela is a country, much like any other, of haves and have-nots. But what marks it out is how willing the haves are to trample on the have-nots – and how far the have-nots are prepared to effect a change in their personal fortunes.

One of the main objectives of making the film was to get access to the Venezuelan prison controlled by Leo (see P is for a Prostitute Called Margarita) and that meant staying in Caracas – at the time of our filming, statistically the most violent capital city on the planet – which meant we had the pleasure of a very nice hotel. For a socialist utopia, there are some very nice hotels in Caracas.

Now, on this particular day I looked out of my window and saw a local guy crossing the road at a pedestrian crossing below. To my horror I saw that even though he seemed to have right of way, a car shot the crossing and knocked him down.

Fortunately, the car wasn't going fast, and relaxing slightly I could see he was only stunned. What's more, there were men rushing out of the car that had knocked him down and going to his aid.

Only, I realised that the occupants of the car weren't trying to help the poor bugger at all. In fact, with practised speed and skill they went through his pockets grabbing anything of value, finally taking his gold Rolex off him before dropping him and jumping back into the car, reversing and roaring off.

It was all over in a few seconds. Dazed, the poor bloke on the floor picked himself up and made his way to safety, and I shook my head thinking that now I'd seen it all. But I hadn't. The next day I saw *exactly the same thing* happen again.

Different victim, of course, and different thieves, too, but exactly the same MO.

That zebra crossing? I gave it a wide berth after that. And I wondered, was it a crashpoint or a cashpoint?

Z is also for Zazazzz

Z is also for Zzzzz . . .

think I've already mentioned that we used to have a saying out in Afghanistan: he who sleeps first sleeps longest. Now if you'll excuse me, I have an appointment with an infected blue mattress, a cuddly toy, a tin of tuna and a lucky ducky. . .